Books

S0-EIL-861

CHARTING THE HERE OF THERE

Books

CHARTING THE HERE OF THERE

French & American Poetry
in Translation in Literary Magazines
1850–2002

Guy Bennett & Béatrice Mousli

THE NEW YORK PUBLIC LIBRARY & GRANARY BOOKS
in association with The Book Office,
Cultural Service of the French Embassy in the United States

NEW YORK CITY 2002

Copyright © 2002 The New York Public Library, Astor, Lenox and Tilden Foundations
and Granary Books
Text copyright © 2002 by Guy Bennett and Béatrice Mousli
All Rights Reserved

Published in conjunction with a symposium sponsored by the French Cultural Services, The New
York Public Library, and the Florence Gould Foundation, held at the Humanities and Social Sciences
Library of The New York Public Library on October 4–6, and an exhibition, *Reviews of Two
Worlds: French-American Literary Periodicals, 1945–2000*, on view at the Library, October
4–December 7, 2002

Exhibitions based on this book will be held at the Doheny Memorial Library, University of Southern
California, February 7–May 9, 2003 with a conference April 4-6; and at the Centre Internationale de
poesie, *Marseille* in the fall of 2003

This publication is made possible by Sue and Edgar Wachenheim III. Support for the Exhibitions
Program at The New York Public Library's Humanities and Social Sciences
Library has been provided by Pinewood Foundation and by Sue and Edgar Wachenheim III

Book and cover design: Julie Harrison
Cover image: *gamma ray burst at the fountain of lust* by Timothy C. Ely, mixed-media
drawing on paper (detail), © 2001, from the collection of Steve Clay.

Library of Congress Cataloging-in-Publication Data

Bennett, Guy
    Charting the here of there : French & American poetry in translation in literary
magazines, 1850-2002 / Guy Bennett & Béatrice Mousli.
        p. cm.
    Includes bibliographical references.
    ISBN 1-887123-63-6 (alk. paper)
    1. French poetry--Translations into English--Periodicals--Bibliography--Exhibitions. 2.
American poetry--Translations into French--Periodicals--Bibliogrpahy--Exhibitions. I.
Mousli, Béatrice. II. Title.

Z2174.P7 B46
[PQ401]

2002032567

The New York Public Library
476 Fifth Avenue
New York, NY 10018
www.nypl.org

Granary Books, Inc.
307 Seventh Ave., Suite 1401
New York, NY 10001
www.granarybooks.com

Distributed to the trade by:
Distributed Art Publishers
155 Avenue of the Americas
New York, NY 10013-1507
Tel: (212) 627-1999
Fax: (212) 627-9484
Orders: (800) 338-BOOK
www.artbook.com

America is too young and Europe too old to produce art, and there you are ... and here I am ...

— MARIUS DE ZAYAS
to Alfred Stieglitz, 1914

Contents

Preface

THERE IS AN UNDENIABLE, yet indefinable bond joining French and American poetry. It can be seen in the ever-increasing numbers of translations published in the two countries, which seem to outnumber works translated from other languages. It is also evident in the shapes and directions taken by the poetry of both nations, which have occasionally overlapped to the point of producing works that, by their very nature, are truly bi-national creations (see, for example, Michael Palmer's translation of Emmanuel Hocquard's *Theory of Tables*, itself, according to Hocquard, a "continuation" of his own translation of Palmer's "Baudelaire Series"). While the reasons for this mutual fascination may be difficult to identify, examples of it are not hard to come by — one need look no further than the pages of literary magazines, where excerpts from an ongoing Franco-American dialogue in poetry are readily apparent.

For the past 150 years, literary magazines have served as the telegraph/telephone/email connection for this dialogue, permitting, with relative speed and facility, the transmission of poetry from one people to the other. The ephemeral, periodic quality of the "little review" has provided a unique forum for the sustained exchange of ideas that continue to inform the writing of French and American poets up to the present day. With the advent of web-based publishing, the products of this exchange have been projected into another dimension, and endowed with a presence and immediacy that seem to erase the real time and space separating the two countries, thus moving their respective poetries even closer.

The goal of this book is to document the high points of this exchange, following it as it writes itself on the pages of French and American literary magazines from 1850 through the present. By documenting the practice of publishing translations in journals, we hope to show how French and American poetry have been perceived historically by writers and readers in both countries, and reveal the many ways in which the two parallel traditions have informed and influenced one another.

The first part of the book is organized chronologically, and divided into six sections that span the 150-year period in question. The first chapter covers the mid- to late-19th century, when Poe and Whitman made their first appearance in France, and French Symbolist and Parnassian poets were being discovered by American readers. The second focuses on the proto-Dada periodicals published in New York by French and American artists and poets in the first two decades of the 20th century. American expatriate magazines and publishers based in 1920s' Paris dominate the third chapter, while the fourth and fifth chapters cover magazine publications in both countries during the 1930s and '40s, '50s, and '60s, respectively.

The final chapter presents the burgeoning literary exchanges of the contemporary period, covering a broad range of publications produced during the years 1970–2002.

In the second part of the book we consider the role of the translator, without whom no exchange would be possible. Rather than produce a documentary-style study, we have chosen to address the issue directly by circulating a brief questionnaire among 18 contemporary French and American translator/poets, and presenting the responses we have received. In their respective contributions, the latter speak of their work, describe their methods and motivations, and discuss the relationship between the poetry they translate and their own writing. Their responses constitute a personal testimony that sheds light on the practice of translation, and demonstrates the ongoing commitment on the part of many French and American writers to a continued bi-national dialogue via poetry.

It goes without saying that we have not attempted to include or even mention every issue of every journal that ever published French or American poetry in translation; that would have been an impossible task. Rather, we have sought to identify magazines that have furthered the dialogue in question by regularly featuring poetry in translation, by drawing attention to that poetry in "special issues" devoted to it, or simply by providing a context in which French and American poets could publish together and thus continue the conversation. This contact has occasionally led to other forms of publication, whether anthologies or chapbook or book series, and this has been duly noted when appropriate.

It is our hope that the present work reveals — if only in part — the rich tradition of literary exchanges that have shaped and informed French and American poetry for more than a century.

— GUY BENNETT & BÉATRICE MOUSLI

Acknowledgments

W<small>E WOULD LIKE TO THANK</small> those individuals and institutions without whom/which this project would have been difficult, if not impossible, to realize:

Emmanuel Ponsart and the staff of the CIPM (centre international de poésie *Marseille*), who graciously made the library collection and Xerox machine available to us, and gave us their support and a variety of important information (such as the address of a fine Moroccan restaurant in Marseilles). Special thanks to Eric Giraud, who promptly answered our many email queries and, with his assistant Sina Riahi, compiled information on French magazines for us.

The many librarians at the University of Southern California, who happily answered our inquiries, and went out of their way to make the inaccessible available to us.

André Chabin and Amal Renne of Ent'revues, who as usual not only supplied us with precious information, but also showed enthusiasm and support for the project.

The following individuals for providing us quasi-instantaneously with detailed information about their respective magazines: Henri Deluy (*Action Poétique*), Jean-Michel Espitallier (*Java*), Claude Royet-Journoud (*Siècle à mains*, *Zuk*, et al.).

Olivier Cariguel and Sophie Robert for their support and for the information they provided.

Andrew Maxwell and Paul Vangelisti, for loaning us rare and otherwise unobtainable magazines from their personal collections.

The poets/translators who took the time to respond to our questionnaire, and without whom this book would be considerably shorter.

Last but not least, much thanks to Yan Brailowsky for offering us this project and being supportive throughout its completion.

— GB & BM
Los Angeles, 2002

1850–1900 / Early Encounters

FRANCO-AMERICAN LITERARY exchanges in the mid-19th century were relatively limited. Few French names ever crossed the Atlantic, and those that did tended to belong to prose writers, not poets. George Sand and Honoré de Balzac had their admirers, but while Alfred de Musset and Victor Hugo (the poet) were recognizable names, they were not popular authors. La Fayette had been forgotten, and the French and American publics seemed more interested in domestic politics than in foreign poetry.

One of the main objectives of American publishers at the time was to free themselves from their cultural dependency on England, in order to prove that they were able to live on their own resources. This was especially true of magazine publishing: for many years, American journals were mere imitations of their British brethren, and the time had come to leave the old model behind and forge a new national voice, none of which was conducive to translations and exchanges. Moreover, poetry was not popular with American editors, and was considered at best acceptable for a female audience.

In France the publishing situation was quite different. Critics showed some interest in American literature, particularly in poetry, but it was the poets themselves who translated their American counterparts and regularly wrote about them. The affinities that Baudelaire and Laforgue felt for Edgar Allan Poe and Walt Whitman were strong enough to compel the former writers to dedicate their time and energy to translating and promoting these American poets; their cause was later taken up by other poets who felt the same compulsion, and like them were eager to share their discoveries. Poe and Whitman, undoubtedly the two strongest influences on late-19th-century French poetry, are wonderful examples of how poetry can be disseminated by a network of translators and little magazines, as we shall see below.

Such was not the case with American magazines, however. Not only did their editors eschew poetry, the very format and layout of American periodicals — often large pages with multiple columns of text — were not especially hospitable to printed verse. In addition, most American magazines then published focused on politics and economics, with relatively few of them interested in literature of any kind.

In 1850, two major American journals existed: the *North American Review*, first published in Iowa in 1815, and *The Literary Messenger, devoted to every department of literature and the fine arts,* founded in 1834 in Richmond, Virginia. Both published literary texts, among other things. Soon they would be followed by a new generation of periodicals. *The International Magazine of Literature, Art, and Science* appeared in 1850, and two years later became *Harper's New Monthly Magazine*, while in 1853 *Putnam's Monthly* appeared, put out by Scribner and Son, the New York publisher. In 1870, *Putnam's Monthly* became *Scribner's Monthly*, finally adopting the title *Scribner's Magazine* in 1887, after a six-year pause in publication. In 1857 *The Atlantic Monthly* was founded in Boston, and in 1869 *Appletons' Journal: A Magazine of General Literature* was first published in New York.

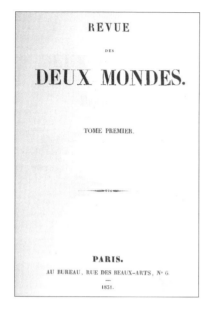

In France, the *Revue des Deux Mondes* had ruled the world of periodicals for decades. Founded in 1832, the *Revue* published articles on politics, travel, philosophy, economics ... and literature. Known for its "serious" writing, the *Revue des Deux Mondes* was widely read, and thus played a role in many aspects of French intellectual life. It had no real competitors until 1844, when the *Revue de Paris* appeared, offering a slightly different point of view on things, but with the same sense of seriousness, and with a similar scope.

Though these two magazines were only marginally interested in literature, such was not the case with the myriad little reviews that were founded after 1870. With the birth of the Third Republic in 1871, French readers watched with amazement as a flourish of little magazines suddenly appeared on the horizon. While most of them were ephemeral, all were driven by the desire to publish contemporary writing, especially that of the Symbolist poets and their followers. They included *La République des Lettres*, founded in 1875 and edited by Catulle Mendès, *Le Décadent* in 1886, *La Plume* and *La Revue Blanche* in 1889, *L'Ermitage* and the *Mercure de France* in 1890, and *La Vogue* in 1899, to mention only the most well-known titles from a list comprising more than a hundred little reviews. They quickly became essential to literary life, as the first — and more often than not, only — place to publish poetry, as Remy de Gourmont remarked in his bibliographical essay, *Les Petites revues*:

> Little magazines were instrumental in bringing writers to the attention of the public. By the end of the 19th century, they had become the chief forum for literary activity in France. As for the importance of little magazines, I shall only say that at no point in their career did Villiers,

Revue des Deux Mondes

Verlaine, Mallarmé or Laforgue ever publish their work anywhere other than in magazines, some of which were so little that their names have been all but forgotten.[1]

Poe in France

> *It is natural that the French (foreigners, unacquainted with American conditions) should be attracted by the SURFACE of his genius and copy the wrong thing, (but the expressive thing), the strange, the bizarre (the recoil) without sensing the actuality, of which that is the complement, — and we get for Poe a reputation for eccentric genius, maimed, the curious, the sick-at-hearts, the unexplainable crop up, unrelated to his ground — which has become his inheritance.*
>
> — WILLIAM CARLOS WILLIAMS
> *In the American Grain*[2]

Williams is a bit harsh on the misguided souls who championed the renegade poet. Among those who were "attracted by the surface of his genius" and copied "the wrong thing" were no less than Charles Baudelaire, Théophile Gauthier, Stéphane Mallarmé, and Paul Valéry, to name the most well-known.

Baudelaire first became aware of Poe's work in the *Revue des Deux Mondes*, in an article by E.D. Forgues (Paul Émile Daurand, 1813–1889). E.D. Forgues was known to promote English authors like Thackeray, Dickens, and George Eliot, and would occasionally devote an essay to American writers such as Nathaniel Hawthorne or Herman Melville. In October 1846, he presented the "Tales of Edgar Allan Poe," introducing his readers to the singular world of the American poet. Though two tales had already been translated the preceding year ("The Purloined Letter" was published anonymously in *Le Magasin Pittoresque*, and "The Descent into the Maelstrom" appeared in *La Revue Britannique*), they went largely unnoticed by the public. It was Forgues's essay and Isabelle Meunier's translation of

E.D. Forgues's "Les Contes d'Edgar A. Poe," *Revue des Deux Mondes*, October (1846).

15

"The Black Cat" (in *La Démocratie Pacifique*, January 1847) that got Baudelaire's attention. The poet was instantly struck by the similarities with his own work, as he later reported to a friend:

> In 1846 or '47 I came across a few fragments by Edgar Poe. I experienced a singular shock. His complete works were not assembled into a single edition until after his death, so I had the patience to make contact with Americans living in Paris to borrow from them collections of newspapers edited by Poe. And then — believe me if you will — I found poems and short stories that I had thought of, but in a vague, confused, and disorderly way and that Poe had been able to bring together to perfection. It was that that lay behind my enthusiasm and my long years of patience.[3]

Baudelaire set about translating the tales and writing an introduction for their publication, a difficult task indeed, considering his relatively poor knowledge of English. He nevertheless persevered, and in July of 1848 "Mesmeric Revelation" was published in the Republican paper *La Liberté de Penser*, and the famous article "Edgar Allan Poe His Life and Work" appeared in the *Revue de Paris* in March and April 1852. A study of the work as well as a tentative biography of the poet, this article became the main source of information for Poe's future French admirers, like Mallarmé or Valéry. Its many good qualities notwithstanding, the article was also the origin of the legend surrounding Poe, since Baudelaire described his life as one long martyrdom, and depicted him as a victim of the "pitiless tyranny of public opinion in democratic societies." The French poet was convinced that "for Poe, the United States was a vast prison through which he wandered with the nervous anxiety of a creature made to breathe the air of a more fragrant world."

Curiously, when it came to translating, Baudelaire limited himself to the tales, arguing that he was not up to translating the poetry: "A translation of such deliberately concentrated poetry can be a beautiful dream, but, unfortunately, it can only be a dream." Thus he invited his readers to discover bits and pieces of the Master's verses in the poems embedded in the tales:

> All that remains is for me to show Poe the poet.... But as any real lover of poetry can tell you, this would be an impossible task. My very humble, very devoted ability as a translator is not sufficient for me to recreate the rhythm and rhyme of Poe's sensuous verse. Perceptive readers should look to the fragments of poems contained in the *Tales*, "The Conqueror Worm" in "Ligeia," and "The Haunted Palace" in "The Fall of the House of Usher," and the mysteriously eloquent "Raven," all of which give glimpses of his extraordinarily pure poetry.[4]

As French readers discovered Poe's works, they found many similarities between the American writer and his French translator, and were quick to conclude that the latter had borrowed from the former. So much so, in fact, that Baudelaire felt it necessary to defend himself, as he explained to a friend in 1864:

> You doubt the truth of this? You doubt that such amazing geometrical parallels can exist in nature? Well, I myself am accused of imitating Edgar Poe! Do you know why I've translated Poe so patiently? Because he was like me. The first time I opened one of his books, I saw, with horror and delight, not only topics I'd dreamed of, but *sentences* I'd thought of, and that he had written twenty years before.[5]

A year later he was still defending himself: "I lost a great deal of time in translating Edgar Poe and the great benefit it brought me was to make some kindly souls say I'd borrowed *my* poems from Poe — poems I'd written ten years before I knew Poe's works."[6] Despite the poet's denials, the legend persisted for decades, as Paul Valéry wrote in his own essay on the "Place of Baudelaire" in French poetry: "I shall merely ask myself what Baudelaire's poetry, and more generally French poetry, may owe to the discovery of the works of Poe. Some poems in *Les Fleurs du Mal* derive their sentiment and their substance from Poe's poems. Some contain lines which are exact transpositions; but I shall ignore these particular borrowings, the importance of which is, in a way, merely local."[7] And he reached the conclusion that more than borrowing, "Baudelaire and Edgar Allan Poe exchanged values. Each gave to the other what he had, and received from the other what he had not."

Whatever critics and readers thought, Poe's works were finally available in France thanks to those publications, as emphasized by Valéry: "This great man would today be completely forgotten if Baudelaire had not taken up the task of introducing him into European literature. Let us not fail to observe here that Poe's universal fame is dimmed or dubious only in his native country and in England. This Anglo-Saxon poet is strangely neglected by his fellow countrymen." For most, Baudelaire's article and translations were the first step toward a deeper knowledge of the American poet.

Thus Paul Verlaine immediately identified with Poe, finding in him an alter ego who believed in "inspiration," and did not view poetry merely as craft, as did most of Verlaine's contemporaries. Verlaine read the tales and Baudelaire's biography when he was very young, and they would inspire one of his first prose pieces, "Le Poteau," published in *Le Hanneton*, in 1867. In that text, he constructs a "conversation with Poe," where a man claims that for many years he was "Edgar Allan Poe's companion in the opium den, and occasionally collaborated with him." Later, when he actually read the poems, he wrote to a friend: "I'm toying with the idea of writing a book of poems.... They will be written according to a system I am working out. They will be very musical, without being puerile, not unlike Poe (what a naïve he was!) I'll tell you more about him some day, for I've read him entirely in *English*."

It is also through Baudelaire that the Parnassian poets came to know the American writer. So closely was the former identified with the latter that Théophile Gauthier, founder of the Parnassian movement, claimed that Baudelaire was better known for his translations of Poe than for his own *Fleurs du Mal*: "more than anything else it was his translation of Edgar Allan Poe that made him famous, for in France we hardly ever read poets, except for their prose works; their poems can only be found in journals."

Gautier considered Baudelaire's translation a success, and judged the critical introduction to be some of the best pages written by the poet:

> Baudelaire's translations of the *Tales of Mystery and Imagination, The Narrative of Arthur Gordon Pym,* and *Eureka* are so exact in both style and thought, evincing a freedom at once scrupulous and supple, that they seem to be original works, and are every bit as perfect as the originals. *The Tales of Mystery and Imagination* are preceded by a critical introduction in which the translator analyzes — from the point of view of a poet — Poe's eccentric and novel talent, which was unknown to the French, with their little regard for innovation from abroad, until Baudelaire revealed it to them. His introduction, which is essential to explain a writer so far removed from common ideas, betrays a rare metaphysical wisdom and refined insight. It contains some of the most remarkable pages he has ever written.[8]

Gautier concluded that "In France, Baudelaire's name will forever be inseparable from that of Edgar Allan Poe, and the thought of one immediately evokes the other. At times it even seems that the ideas of the American poet rightfully belong to his French counterpart." Like many other Parnassian poets (Leconte de Lisle, for example, whose "Raven" reminds readers of its famous American counterpart), Gautier recognized the debt he himself owed the author of the *Tales*.

Poe's translators and critics became more and more numerous throughout this period; by the end of the 19th century, Gustave Kahn, Stéphane Mallarmé, and Armand Renaud had been added to the list. On August 1, 1864, Renaud published a long article in the *Revue de Paris*, entitled "Edgar Poe d'après ses poésies," followed by translations of some of Poe's most important poems. Renaud was a friend of Mallarmé who, according to legend, learned English in order to read the American writer. By 1864 Mallarmé already considered Poe his "Master," as he wrote to his friend Henri Cazalis: "The more I go on, the more faithful I shall be to the severe ideas bequeathed to me by my Master, Edgar Allan Poe."

But despite his early interest in Poe, Mallarmé published no translations until the summer of 1872, when a few appeared in *La Renaissance littéraire et artistique*. He felt he had a mission to accomplish, and a debt to pay to Baudelaire's legacy, as he stated to Villiers de L'Isle-Adam in October 1867: "I have inherited this task from Baudelaire."[9] He published further translations nine years later in *La République des Lettres* (a magazine edited by his friend and mentor Catulle Mendès). Meanwhile, in an early example of poetic energy coursing between the two nations, Mallarmé's "Tombeau d'Edgar Poe" was translated in October 1875 and read at the unveiling ceremony of a monument to Poe in Baltimore that same month.

Mallarmé felt his English was too limited to handle Poe's effusive vocabulary, and though, unlike Baudelaire, he did in fact translate Poe's poems, he was reluctant to take on any of his other writings. For this reason, he declined a job as translator for Hachette, the French publishing house, when Mendès offered him the position in March 1871: "The only words of English I know are contained in Poe's poetry, and I pronounce them correctly so as not to betray his meter. With a dictionary and a bit of divination I can be a good translator, especially for poets, which is rare; but that is not enough for a position with Hachette."[10]

When in October of 1890 a young Paul Valéry introduced himself — in the third person — to "the Master" (in his case, Mallarmé), he used the name "Edgar Allan Poe" as a password:

> By means of a brief introduction, he must declare that he prefers short, concentrated poems of dazzling effect, poems whose rhythms are like marmoreal steps leading to the altar wreathed with the last verse! But he is deeply imbued with the knowing doctrines of the great Edgar Allan Poe, who is perhaps the most subtle artist of the century! This name alone should suffice to give you an idea of his Poetics.[11]

Some twenty years later, when he spoke of reading Poe, Valéry told the critic Albert Thibaudet: "He gave me what I needed, taken as I was with the frenzied lucidity he conveys."[12]

Like his predecessor, Valéry would pay his tribute to Poe by translating some of his works. He chose the "Marginalia," which he published in *Commerce* in the fall of 1927, presenting his translation and commentary side by side. The few lines of introduction that Valéry wrote for this project show that he accepted the image Baudelaire had given of the American *poète maudit*:

> I do not know in what circumstances Poe was led to publish the Marginalia. It is not hard for me to imagine. The preamble in which he introduces them breathes the embarrassment of the author and seems to be a kind of excuse, or special plea, for a publication he would probably not even have thought of undertaking, had not some critical phase in his

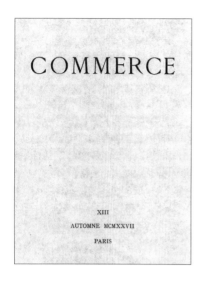

COMMERCE

XIII

AUTOMNE MCMXXVII

PARIS

hapless fortunes forced him, in spite of himself, to print and give to the public these crumbs of his thought. ... He scattered them at diverse periods in the *Messenger*, the *Philadelphia Democratic Review*, *Graham's Magazine* ... Publications of this kind make me think of the story of a man whose sled is being pursued by a pack of starving wolves. To gain time and distance he throws them everything he has with him. He begins with the least precious.[13]

Though it is difficult to say whether Valéry had a high opinion of this text or not, he did translate it, leaving copious annotations in the margins, and thus engaging in a dialogue with the late Poe.

Salut au Monde!

In search of further innovation, the Symbolists turned from Poe to another American: Walt Whitman. In 1855 the Poet of Camden had published a ground-breaking work whose title was puzzling to French readers: *Leaves of Grass*. Singing the world, the people, the values of democracy, Whitman appeared as a liberator to French poets. Not only were his themes unconventional, his poetry was also free of constraint, and its rhythm was exhilarating.

The first critics to show interest in the American poet were Louis Étienne, whose article "Walt Whitman, poète philosophe et *rowdy*" was published in November 1861 in *La Revue Européenne*, and Thérèse Bentzon and Émile Blémont, who almost simultaneously brought Whitman to French readers in June 1872, Bentzon in the *Revue des Deux Mondes* ("Un poète américain — Walt Whitman; 'Muscle and Pluck Forever'"), and Blémont in *La Renaissance littéraire et artistique* ("La poésie en Angleterre et aux États-Unis").

Later critics would denounce these articles, reproaching them for their naïveté and their lack of understanding of the work. One of Whitman's most ardent French supporters summed up his criticism of the critics thus:

UN

POÈTE AMÉRICAIN

WALT WHITMAN.

Muscle and pluck for ever!

« N'avez-vous pas, disait dernièrement un critique anglais, n'avez-vous pas entendu parler de la musique de l'avenir? n'avez-vous pas entendu la musique elle-même? Ce n'est plus une chose promise, c'est un fait accompli, du moins les fondations seules sont déjà proclamées par certains prophètes supérieurs aux plus hauts sommets qu'aient atteints ces talens médiocres du passé : Mozart, Haendel, Beethoven! Il en est de même de la poésie de l'avenir : ses chants sont annoncés, et le premier chanteur se tient là parmi nous. A la vérité il n'est que le précurseur d'une longue série de poètes futurs, mais ceux-ci marcheront sur ses pas, comme Virgile sur ceux d'Homère, Dante sur ceux de Virgile, Milton sur ceux de Dante, et ainsi de suite, l'héritage sacré se transmettant de main en main... Le vieux monde est fini , mais Apollon a choisi les États-Unis pour refuge, et la pauvre petite fontaine d'Hippocrène vient d'être remplacée par les flots bruyans de l'intarissable Mississipi, l'Hélicon et le Parnasse ont abdiqué en faveur des Alleghanys et du soleil levant. » Le poète de l'avenir dont M. Austin annonce ainsi l'apparition avec une ironie attristée n'est point connu en France; jusqu'en 1867, il ne l'était en Angleterre que par les sévères critiques de quelques journaux, échos fidèles d'une bonne partie de la presse américaine, et les citations produites à l'appui

top: *Commerce*, no. 13 (1927).
bottom: Thérèse Bentzon's essay, "Poete Americain Walt Whitman," in the *Revue des Deux*

> You can see the old habits shocked by this new work, you can see the
> beginning of his influence. Some of these articles are truly bad: such blind-
> ness, such lack of understanding is astonishing. But they are not without
> interest because they occasionally say the exact opposite of what
> Whitman's work really is, and in so doing, they help us — the enormity of
> their error reveals the truth. One such article (perhaps the first in France)
> appeared in the *Revue des Deux Mondes* on June 1, 1872. The epigraph
> announces the author's misinterpretation: "Muscle and Pluck forever."[14]

According to Valery Larbaud, author of the above lines, the critics had creat-
ed an image of the American poet that reflected what they wanted to see in him,
and not necessarily what he was: "They have created Whitman the Prophet,
Whitman the Worker, Whitman the Philosopher."[15]

Though the portrait they painted was not as accurate as it might have been,
it was precisely those articles that made Whitman's name known in France. When,
in the early 1880s, Jules Laforgue read the essay published in the *Revue des Deux
Mondes*, he was immediately drawn to this poet who
allowed himself to write in *vers libre*, and treated themes
that were not commonly found in the poetry of the time.

Laforgue would soon find a copy of the book and
begin translating it. His goal was to render the entire
work into French and publish it with a biographical and
critical introduction, in essence doing for Whitman what
Baudelaire had done for Poe. In June 1886, under the
title of "Brins d'herbe: traduit de l'étonnant poète améri-
cain Walt Whitman," eight poems were published in *La
Vogue*, the Symbolist magazine edited by Gustave Kahn.
La Vogue ran more of Laforgue's translations in July and
August of the same year, but the project ended with the
sudden death of the translator. The American-born poet
Francis Viélé-Griffin hoped to pick up where Laforgue
had left off, and wrote Whitman, requesting the right to
translate the American edition of *Leaves of Grass* — not the "ridiculously expur-
gated" version, as he put it, published in England by Chatto & Windus. Once
again the project never materialized, but Viélé-Griffin did submit translations to
every magazine he knew; in 1888, a first translation appeared in the *Revue
Indépendante*, followed by others in *La Cravache Parisienne* (1889), *Les
Entretiens Politiques et Littéraires* (1892), and *L'Ermitage* (1899).

The 1908 publication of a biography of Whitman by Léon Bazalgette (*Walt

---

Léon Bazalgette's translation of *Leaves of Grass* (1909).

Whitman, l'homme et son œuvre), and a complete translation of *Leaves of Grass* by the same author the following year, firmly established the American poet as a major figure of modern poetry in France. Though many critics found fault with Bazalgette's treatment and presentation of Whitman, they all admired his devotion to the author of *Leaves of Grass*, and were grateful for his work. Praise came from all sides, with perhaps the most ardent supporter of Bazalgette being the writer and critic Valery Larbaud, who warmly welcomed the translation in an article published in *La Phalange* in April of 1909: "Our great Comrade finally speaks to us in French." His acclaim notwithstanding, Larbaud was not uncritical of Bazalgette, reproaching him for one major shortcoming: the latter's attempt to purge Whitman's poems of any allusion to his homosexuality: "It said *Love* in the text. Were you afraid of the sniggering of fools?"

This issue of Whitman's sexuality was still very divisive among the *Whitmaniens*, with some, like Stuart Merrill, choosing to deny it, and others, like André Gide, viewing the American poet as a spokesman for the cause. In the middle, critics like Larbaud or Guillaume Apollinaire were simply interested in stating the facts and giving the most accurate possible portrait of the American poet. At one point Apollinaire provoked an argument with Merrill when, in his article "Les funérailles de Walt Whitman racontées par un témoin," he wrote:

> The homosexuals were out in full force, the most popular being a beautiful young man of some twenty years of age: Peter Conelly, an Irish streetcar conductor originally working in Washington, then later in Philadelphia, whom Whitman especially loved.

Attacked by Stuart Merrill, he responded that "unisexuality" (the term he used for homosexuality) was not only as common in the United States as it was in Europe, but that revealing celebrated artists and intellectuals to be "unisexual" could only help fight those who found homosexuality unlawful:

> Since the discriminatory and barbaric legislation of certain states viciously condemns unisexuals, doesn't M. Merrill feel it would be in the best interest to show that among unisexuals there have been many men of genius? Wouldn't the prestige of the latter men help undo the cruelty and inequity of the laws quoted by M. Merrill?

"To fight prejudice" is how Gide saw it, as he explained in *Corydon*, where a mask of Whitman's face is displayed on Doctor Corydon's desk. This statement was symbolic of being under the protection of the "old man with a great white beard." However, by the time *Corydon* was published in 1924 the controversy had more or less died down, and though prejudice against homosexuals had certainly not disappeared, the sexual preferences of the American poet were no longer an issue.

Interest in Whitman never really diminished. His influence reached beyond Symbolist circles, touching other "schools" or movements such as Unanimism, for example. The 1918 publication of Whitman's *Œuvres Choisies*, which presented in book form many of the translations previously published in magazines, helped renew interest in the American poet. Subsequently, in March 1926 the Montpellier-based *Âne d'Or* published a special issue dedicated to Whitman, with essays by Léon Bazalgette and Pierre Berger, and translations of poems and notes by Jean Catel and R. Martin, and the Parisian *Navire d'Argent* published the "Dix-huitième présidence," translated by Jean Catel, a text that would be published in book form two years later by *Tambour*. From April to June, at the initiative of the Comité Walt Whitman, whose president was none other than Francis Viélé-Griffin, an exhibit was organized at the famous American bookstore on the Left Bank, Shakespeare and Company. The goal of the organizers was to interest the French public in

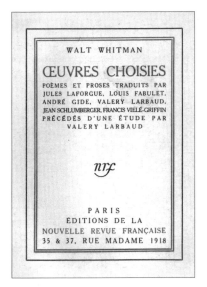

Whitman and raise money to be sent to New York as a contribution for the construction of a Whitman monument. Sylvia Beach, the owner of the bookstore, displayed Whitman memorabilia owned by her family, and also exhibited French and American magazines that had published the poet, as well as various book editions of his work.

French intellectuals had always seen Walt Whitman as the Bard of democracy and freedom. In 1943, his words became both prophetic and uplifting, so much so that they were reproduced as a dedication of that year's issue of *Message*, a magazine published in Geneva and Paris by the Editions des Trois Collines:

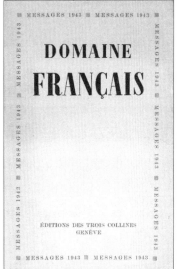

> O star of France!
> The brightness of thy hope and strength and fame,
> Like some proud ship that led the fleet so long,
> Beseems to-day a wreck driven by the gale, a mastless hulk,
> And 'mid its teeming madden'd, half drown'd crowds,

---

top: Whitman's *Selected Work* in French translation, edited by Larbaud (1918).
bottom: *Messages* (1943).

Nor helm nor helmsman.
Dim, smitten star! ...
Star crucified! by traitors sold!
Star panting o'er a land of death — heroic land!
Strange, passionate, mocking, frivolous land.

It was undoubtedly difficult for many of those who read these lines to imagine that they had been written between 1870 and 1880, as tribute to another war.

Following in the footsteps of their predecessors, a number of contemporary poets and translators collaborated on a special issue of the magazine *Poésie*, entitled "Walt Whitman, le passeur," which was published in December 1991. In addition to critical articles, the issue includes pieces by seven contemporary French writers (namely, Daniel Biga, Xavier Bordes, François de Cornière, Jacques Darras, Petr Král, André Velter, and Franck Venaille) responding to the work of the American poet. Also featured is a discussion between poet/translator Jacques Darras and Scottish writer Kenneth White on Whitman's modernity and relevance at the end of the 20th century.

French Poetry in American Magazines

I recall how, when I used to long for a glimpse of the Old World, my parents would quote to me the railway advertising slogan: See America First. ... in the last decades of the nineteenth and the early years of the past century they did not care for cosmopolitans, and even the more cultivated were inclined to reprove or to lament Henry James.
— SAMUEL PUTNAM,
Paris Was Our Mistress

While the French were inspired by American poets, it seems that the contrary was not true; at least, that is the impression given by American magazines of the period. In general, they showed little interest in and knowledge of what was happening in France at the time, and seem distinctly reactionary when compared to their French counterparts. This could even be seen in the respective magazine formats of the two countries: most American periodicals were still being laid out as newspapers, whereas in the second half of the 19th century, France witnessed the birth of the literary magazine such as it is known today, with pages dedicated to poetry, articles, and reviews. In America, when pages were reserved for the writing of a single poet, like Alphonse de Lamartine or Victor Hugo, they usually were filled with critical analyses of the work in question, within which excerpts from poems were quoted in translation.

Furthermore, critics tended to be conservative, and always maintained a certain distance from their subject, as if French poetry were somehow unsuitable for American readers. On various occasions, critics strongly expressed their disapproval of French literary trends, as in the following conclusion of a long article published in April 1837 in the *North American Review* (vol. 44, issue 95), simply titled "Modern French Poetry":

> We hope we have succeeded in showing, that there is at present no dearth of poetical talent in France. It is indeed, perverted by corrupt taste, and clouded by gross fault. The prevalence of dramatic production and the eagerness with which the populace throng to witness exhibitions hideously immoral, but sustained by the vitiated tastes and political passions of the multitude, have exerted the most pernicious effect both on their writers and the public. But such minds as that of M. de Lamartine cannot be without their influence; and we may therefore hope that a change in this respect, as complete as the recent one from the monotonous formality of the old school, will before long take place.

And the poets chosen to illustrate modern French poetry were Casimir Delavigne, Lamartine, and Béranger, two Romantics and a *chansonnier*.

In 1850, Americans were treated to the following comments on French poetry, taken from a review of a *Choix de Poésie* destined for those learning the language, printed in *The Southern Quarterly Review* of July 1850:

> As a means of exercising the youthful learner in the acquisition of the French language, this will prove no doubt an excellent volume. The selections are made with good taste, and show much judgment in the employment of such pieces, as, properly simple, will gradually conduct the learner to a just appreciation of the peculiarities of the French idiom, and the caprices of the language, without distressing memory and attention too much at the outset. We have no great faith in, or admiration for the French poetry, for any purpose, and do but commend this as an agent of instruction in language, and not as calculated either to wing the imagination, or greatly elevate the soul. The book is very nicely prepared, with externals quite worthy of the contents, neither being inappropriate to the delicate hands of the young lady-learners, for whom both are designed.

In 1869, the leading poets of the "New Generation" were still Casimir Delavigne, Lamartine, and Béranger, but new figures were on the horizon: Victor Hugo, whose *Autumn Leaves* were thought in 1837 to "hardly prove as fugitive as their name would indicate," Alfred de Musset, and "possibly Baudelaire"[16] found a place in that narrow pantheon. Of the three, Hugo and Lamartine inspired the most commentary. For American critics, Lamartine was "one of the purest representatives of French poetry of the nineteenth century,"[17] whereas Victor Hugo was a "literary Titan,"[18] and was richly eulogized when he died. However, while critics showed some interest in the "Titans," that is, in the most well-known, though certainly not the most revolutionary writers, there was little or nothing said about the forward-looking, innovative poetry being written in France at the time. Baudelaire was mentioned only in passing, and the names of Paul Verlaine, Arthur Rimbaud, Jules Laforgue, and Lautréamont were nowhere to be found.

The poetry of the last forty years of the century seemed to be of no interest; perhaps it was too far removed from any frame of reference for most American critics to appreciate. On the other hand, prose and drama traveled better than poetry, and were more in favor with the public, which actually led the critics to diminish the importance of any poetic movement: "The great authors of this century in France have been writers of prose — philosophers, historians, novelists and critics — and comparatively little of the poetry produced has made itself heard beyond the boundaries of the nation."[19]

In March 1893, however, *Scribner's Magazine* published a groundbreaking article, entitled "The French Symbolists," by Aline Gorren. For the first time, Stéphane Mallarmé, Paul Verlaine, Arthur Rimbaud, Jean Moréas, and Gustave Kahn — "the high priests and chief glories of the Symbolist movement" — were presented to American readers, as were Maurice Barrès, Francis Poictevin, and Paul Adam, whom the author considered to be leaders of Symbolist prose. While the latter were widely published in book form, the former depended mostly on the ephemeral life of small magazines, as Gorren emphasized:

About the year 1885 that section of the Parisian public that concerns itself with special departments of letters, became conscious of the existence of sundry obscure little reviews, formulating a new aesthetic creed, in a language departing, as far as it was possible to go from the phrase of Zola, Daudet, Maupassant. ... The little reviews generally died out, within a period of varying brevity, for lack of readers and funds. But others sprang up in their place, and propagated the new dogmas further.

Aline Gorren's article on "The French Symbolists," *Scribner's Magazine* (1893).

Though the article contained excerpts of poems, there was not a single complete translation, and the reader was left to his own devices when it came to finding and reading — most probably in the original — the poetry discussed by the author.

Unfortunately, if magazine articles were already scarce, books were even scarcer, Lamartine and Hugo being the only two poets that could claim a volume published in the United States. Other editions existed of course, published in London for the most part, but the almost total absence of American translations is indicative of the little interest taken in French poetry in the United States at the time. As for France in general, judging from echoes in the press, American newspapers were more likely to report on England or Germany than France, though ties between the two nations had been strong during the Revolutionary War. After Lafayette's visit to the new state in 1824, the relationship between the two countries seemed to wither, with indifference, at least on the part of Americans, being the dominant tone.

The lack of curiosity with respect to things French was not to last, however. The first years of the 20th century saw a renewal of interest on the part of many Americans in what was happening in Paris, where a "new art" was being elaborated. That new art would make its presence felt at the 1913 Armory Show in New York, where work by Matisse, Picabia, Duchamp, and others experienced a *succès de scandale* that would forever change the perception of "Modern Art" in America. The change was not due to the Armory Show alone, as by that time certain American poets and artists had been paving the way for the introduction of European Modernism into the United States for nearly a decade. Foremost among them was American photographer Alfred Stieglitz, who ran a small gallery at 291 Fifth Avenue in New York. It quickly became a haven for a number of forward-looking European artists, many of whom had their first American show there. It also served as the headquarters for the first Modernist journals published in the United States, as we shall see in the following chapter.

Notes

[1] Unless otherwise noted, all translations from the French are my own. — GB.
[2] Williams, p. 223.
[3] Baudelaire, 1986, p. 203.

[4]*Cahiers Jacques Doucet* (1934).
[5]Baudelaire, 1975, p. 204.
[6]Ibid., p. 221.
[7]Valéry, 1972, p. 170.
[8]Baudelaire, 1923, p. 38.
[9]Baudelaire, 1975, p. 725.
[10]Ibid., p. 1535.
[11]Valéry, 1952, pp. 28–29.
[12]Ibid., p. 97.
[13]Valéry, 1972, p. 177.
[14]Larbaud, p. 336.
[15]Larbaud, p. 221.
[16]*Putnam's Magazine* 14.22 (October 1869): 512.
[17]*Overland Monthly and Out West Magazine* 1.4 (April 1883): 368.
[18]*Overland Monthly and Out West Magazine* 6.33 (July 1885): 82.
[19]*Putnam's Magazine* 14.22 (October 1869): 512.

1900–1920 / Paris, NY

> *For some time I have been working to establish artistic connections between Europe and America, for I believe that the only way to succeed in maintaining the evolutionary progress of modern ideas is through the interchange of ideas among all peoples.*
>
> — MARIUS DE ZAYAS
> *to Tristan Tzara*

INTERESTINGLY ENOUGH, the periodicals we today consider manifestations of "American Dada" have their roots not in European literary journals, but in the New York-based photography magazine *Camera Work*, edited by Alfred Stieglitz. Founded in 1903 in order to promote Stieglitz's Photo-Secession, *Camera Work* appeared in a total of fifty issues before ceasing publication in 1917. During that time, it underwent somewhat of a transformation. Though it had been created to promote the ideals and activities of the Photo-Secession, in 1909 the scope of *Camera Work* broadened to include essays on art and aesthetics, thereby presenting Stieglitz's vision of photography as a valid medium for artistic expression in a context more likely to affirm it.

A sampling of these essays is revealing in that it demonstrates Stieglitz's commitment to the promotion of modern art in America; they include: "Henri Matisse and Isadora Duncan" by Charles H. Caffin (no. 25, 1909); "That Toulouse-Lautrec Print!" by S.H. (no. 29, 1910); three articles on Rodin by Benjamin de Casseres, Agnes Ernst Meyer, and S.H.; "A Note on Paul Cézanne" by Charles H. Caffin; "Pablo Picasso" by Marius de Zayas (nos. 34/35, 1911); "The Unconscious in Art" by Benjamin de Casseres (no. 36, 1911); an excerpt from Bergson's *Creative Evolution* (no. 36, 1911); an excerpt from *Concerning the Spiritual in Art* by Kandinsky (no. 39, 1912); a Special Issue on Matisse and Picasso, by Gertrude Stein (1912); and "Aphorisms on Futurism" by Mina Loy (no. 44, 1913). More than merely publish articles about the above artists, Stieglitz actually brought their work to the American public, exhibiting it at The Little Galleries of the Photo-Secession at 291 Fifth Avenue. Artists who had shows at "291," as the gallery came to be known, include Brancusi, Cézanne, Arthur Dove, John Marin, Man Ray, Matisse, Georgia O'Keeffe, Picasso, Rodin, Gino Severini, Toulouse-Lautrec, and Max Weber, for several of whom this was their first exhibit in the United States.

In 1914 Stieglitz considered abandoning "291" in the hope that a new generation would take over. As if seeking advice, he asked friends to write him a note stating what the gallery meant to them, and he published their responses in *Camera Work* 47 (1915). He must have been encouraged, for he did publish three more issues of the magazine over the next two years, ceasing publication in 1917. Among those who responded to his call were a number of well-known artists and writers, many of whom would later become affiliated with the New York Dada group: Adolf Wolff (who later that year would be published in Man Ray's first magazine, *The Ridgefield Gazook*), Alfred Kreymborg (who later co-founded the magazine *Others* with Walter Arensberg), Djuna Barnes, Marsden Hartley (who would have work in *New York Dada*), Arthur G. Dove, Man Ray (who would edit

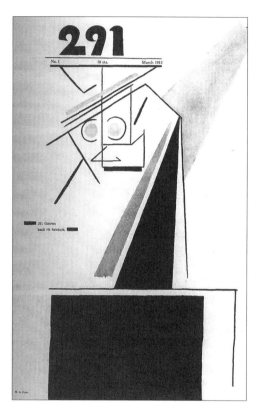

various Dada magazines), Edward Steichen, Francis Picabia, and Marius de Zayas.

de Zayas was a Mexican caricaturist who had settled in New York City in 1907. Stieglitz, who was interested in caricatures, had heard of his work, sought him out, and was sufficiently impressed to exhibit twenty-five of his caricatures at a show at "291" in 1909. The two became friends, and de Zayas began contributing to *Camera Work*, writing articles on the Parisian art scene, the relationship between photography and art, caricature, and aesthetic theory. Perhaps more importantly, he was instrumental in bringing Stieglitz into contact with the work of the European avant-garde, traveling to Paris in 1910 and again in 1914 to meet artists and writers such as Picasso and Apollinaire, and encouraging Stieglitz to show and publish their work in the United States. In a letter written from Paris on July 9, 1914, de Zayas declared to his friend:

I am working hard in making these people understand the convenience of a commerce of ideas with America. And I want to observe the spirit of what they are doing to bring it to "291." We need a closer contact with Paris, there is no question about it.[1]

291, no. 1 (1915).

When Stieglitz contemplated abandoning his role of champion of modern art in America, de Zayas stepped in, co-founding a magazine with Paul B. Haviland, an associate of Stieglitz's, and later opening The Modern Gallery, which would carry on the work of "291." The magazine, named *291* in honor of Stieglitz's gallery, published its first issue in March 1915, and The Modern Gallery opened with an exhibit of work by Georges Braque, Francis Picabia, Pablo Picasso, Alfred Stieglitz, and a selection of African sculpture in October of that same year.

291 was in a sense the prototypical Dada journal, except, of course, that Dada did not yet exist. Approximately one year before Dada was founded in Zurich and the first Dada magazine was published (*Cabaret Voltaire*, May 1916), *291* produced the model for the Dada periodical in New York. It featured a blend

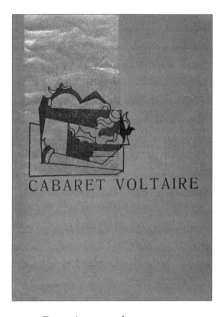

of art, poetry, and polemics that were the standard mix of the Modernist magazine. It was printed on fine paper in a large format (approximately 12 x 20 inches), utilizing the exploratory typographic design and layout that would become staples of Dadaist visual language. *291* appeared in a total of nine issues (six single and three double issues), the final one dating from February 1916.

In addition to de Zayas, whose drawings, critical texts, and poems are featured in each issue, contributors included Apollinaire, whose "Voyages" was the first calligramme to be published in the United States; Stieglitz, who is represented by a brief text and the photograph entitled "Steerage"; Picasso and Braque, whose drawings and paintings were featured; Alberto Savinio, who contributed a musical composition (a chorale by Satie was also to be published in *291*); Georges Ribemont-Dessaignes, who contributed a poem called "musique"; Max Jacob, whose chronicle of life in the French capital entitled "La Vie Artistique" appears in the last two issues; and Francis Picabia, whose texts and drawings — including the first "machine-style" drawings — appear in five of the nine issues. In fact, issue 5–6 from July–August 1915 is a special issue/portfolio of five mechanistic "portraits" done in this new style: the first of Stieglitz, another of de Zayas, Paul Haviland, "a Young American Girl in a State of Nudity," and a self-portrait.

These portraits were inspired by an epiphany that Picabia experienced upon his return to the United States in June 1915, when he came to the realization that

Cabaret Voltaire, first and only issue (1916).

"the genius of the modern world is machinery."[2] This was Picabia's second stay in New York (he had previously come to the U.S. to attend the Armory Show in 1913, where his work was exhibited), and he would remain one full year before setting off for Spain. Settling in Barcelona, he frequented the French expatriate community of artists which included Marie Laurencin, Albert Gleizes, Maximilien Gautier (Max Goth), Valentine de Saint-Point, Serge Charchoune, and Arthur Cravan. He was befriended by José Dalmau, a young gallerist who was taken with French art and who had actually exhibited Picabia's work in his gallery. Having seen a copy of *291* that Picabia had brought with him from New York, Dalmau suggested that Picabia found a new magazine in Barcelona, which he did, calling it *391*.

As Michel Sanouillet would write, "By titling his magazine *391*, Picabia was implicitly recognizing the paternity of *291* and committing himself to take up the work begun by de Zayas and Haviland in their magazine."[3] What *391* owed to *291* could be seen in more than just the title. The two magazines shared roughly the same large format, layout, and typeface. As Sanouillet has noted, even the publication information printed on the back cover of *391* was modeled on that of *291*. "In short," he concludes, "when Picabia first thought of publishing a magazine in Barcelona, he apparently gave Oliva de Vilanova (Dalmau's printer) a hastily made layout based on the last issue of *291*."[4]

All material and graphic similarities notwithstanding, there were some fundamental differences between the two magazines. *291* was more visually driven, with its many reproductions of paintings and photographs, and was more openly experimental in nature, as was most evident in de Zayas's "psychotypes," typographically exploratory poems not unlike Italian Futurist *parole in libertà* or Apollinaire's *calligrammes*, on which they were modeled. In comparison, *391* is a quieter, more writerly magazine which, though it did feature artwork (mostly drawings by Picabia himself), seems more of a literary than an art journal. Commenting on this quality, Francis Naumann has noted that:

> Even though named in an obvious homage to *291*, the magazine bore little resemblance to its predecessor. From the very first issue, Picabia envisioned his magazine as a more ephemeral publication, a personal forum that was intended to preserve the spirit of *291* without any effort to duplicate its printed quality.[5]

Indeed, *391* can be seen as the intermittent diary of its editor, covering seven of the most active and productive years of Picabia's career. The magazine followed him both geographically and aesthetically, from Barcelona where it was founded to New York, then later to Zurich and Paris, reflecting his evolution as a painter and poet from the mechanistic, post-Cubist work of the mid-1910s to the Dadaist

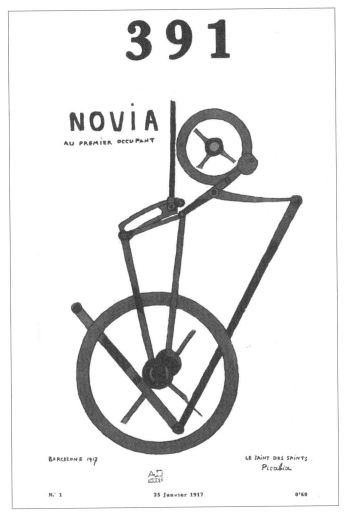

drawings and poetry of the late '10s and early '20s. The final issue of *391*, published in October 1924, heralded the advent of *Instantanéisme*, a hyperephemeral (sham?) movement intended, it would seem, to be a polemical thorn in the side of the nascent Surrealist movement, whose founding manifesto was published the same month.

391 was generally a slim affair, rarely longer than six pages in length. It has a personal, almost intimate feel to it, though it was far from a vanity publication. While Picabia was undoubtedly its most prolific contributor, *391* featured the work of a wide variety of artists and writers, and its list of contributors reads like a who's who of the early 20th century avant-garde: Apollinaire, Arp, Breton,

391, no. 1, January (1917).

Cocteau, Cravan, Desnos, Duchamp, Eluard, Gleizes, Max Jacob, Magritte, Man Ray, Pound, Ribemont-Dessaignes, Satie, Soupault, and Tzara, to name but a few.

Picabia returned to New York in April 1917, for what would be his third and final visit to the United States. During his ten-month stay, he produced three issues of *391*. They are beautifully and minimally designed, and their similar covers and page layouts give them a visual coherence that makes them stand out among the other issues of this seminal magazine. In New York, Picabia was part of a bohemian circle of artists and intellectuals made up of a combination of French expatriates and Americans, including Arthur Cravan, Marcel Duchamp, Albert Gleizes, Edgard Varèse, Henri-Pierre Roché, Walter Arensberg, Isadora Duncan, Alfred Stieglitz, Beatrice Wood, and Marius de Zayas. The pages of *391* reflect the eclectic personality of this Franco-American group, many of whom were contributors.

The first New York issue (no. 5), entitled "Âne," contains prose pieces, poems, and drawings by Picabia, a prose piece and a poem by Varèse, a verbal caricature by de Zayas, two poems by Walter Arensberg (the only pieces in English), and an essay on modern painting by Gleizes. The final page presents chronicles of life in Paris, by Max Jacob, and Barcelona, by Picabia (under the pseudonym of Pharamousse), and brief statements on Picabia's New York circle of friends (de Zayas, Duchamp, Cravan, Gleizes, et al.). The following issue (no. 6), entitled "Américaine," contains five poems and two portraits (one of Duchamp, the other of a matador), all by Picabia. In addition to a rambling poem by Paul-Émile Bibily, the French Vice-Consul at the time, and an odd, essay-like piece on the cinematographer by one Henry J. Vernot, the final New York issue of *391* (no. 7), "Ballet Mécanique," includes poems and a drawing by Picabia, and a prose piece entitled "Chess Game between Picabia and Roché" by Arensberg, which Sanouillet sees as a sort of *écriture automatique avant la lettre*.[6]

Sanouillet also suggests that the chess game referred to in Arensberg's piece could be the match whose outcome determined the fate of the magazine *The Blindman*, which many consider to be the first "official" Dada publication in America, though the label "Dada" was not yet being applied to the group affiliated with the magazine or to its activities. According to legend, Picabia and Henri-Pierre Roché, one of the editors of *The Blindman*, had wagered the future of their respective magazines on a chess game. Picabia is said to have won, and Roché shut down *The Blindman*.

The Blindman was one of the many short-lived magazines that would come to characterize the New York Dada scene. Edited by Marcel Duchamp, Henri-Pierre Roché, and Beatrice Wood, it knew only two issues. The first was published to coincide with the opening of the First Exhibition of the Society of Independent Artists on April 10, 1917, and the second one month later when Duchamp resigned from the organization he had helped found.

The inaugural issue of *The Blindman* was intended to present the Society of Independent Artists to the public and herald its first exhibition. It opens with a lengthy editorial by Roché, organized — in manifesto style — into twenty-three numbered, aphoristic statements relating the founding and goals of the SIA. This is followed by three fanciful prose sketches by Beatrice Wood, and concludes with a brief essay by Mina Loy, who was doubtful that the SIA would be able to successfully "educate the public" with respect to modern art. All in all, the first issue of *The Blindman* is rather tame by Dada standards, but did achieve its goal of introducing the Independents to the public, who were able to purchase a copy at the exhibit for only ten cents.

The second issue (called *The Blind Man*) is much more provocative in tone and polemical in intent, published as it was on the heels of Duchamp's contentious resignation from the SIA when the urinal he submitted (under the pseudonym R. Mutt and the title *Fountain*) was rejected from the exhibit. The issue focuses on that event, and considerable discussion is given to it, chiefly in the form of an essay by Louise Norton ("The Richard Mutt Case") who dubbed the porcelain readymade "Buddha of the Bathroom." *The Blind Man* also contains poetry by Arensberg, Picabia, and Charles Duncan, among others, prose pieces by Erik Satie and Mina Loy, and a brief essay on Marie Laurencin by Gabrielle Buffet (Picabia's wife). Clara Tice contributed a pen and ink portrait of Varèse, Joseph Stella a painting entitled *Coney Island*, and Stieglitz a photograph of the famous urinal, which he also exhibited at "291." The cover features Duchamp's elegant *Chocolate Mill*.

Two months after the second and final issue of *The Blindman*, Duchamp, Roché, and Wood again joined forces to found a new magazine, this one more ephemeral than the last. *Rongwrong* — whose title is said to have been the result of a printer's error — existed in a single issue. While it lacks the polemical punch of its predecessor and seems almost conventional in comparison, one does suspect a bit of tomfoolery here and there, especially in the pseudonymous presence of "Marcel Douxami" and "Marquis de la Torre."

The Blindman, no.1 (1917).

Rongwrong opens with a mock "letter to the editor" by M. Douxami, criticizing *391* and attacking Picabia ("Our Picabia would make an excellent industri-

RONGWRONG

al designer ..." "As for his literature ... Picabia's little charades aren't excessively nasty ..."). It is followed by a response in verse by Picabia, a brief play (in French) and a prose piece (in English) by Carl Van Vechten, and Dada/Surrealist-style "proverbs" by Robert Carlton Brown and Allen Norton, among other writings. Artwork was provided by Edith Clifford Williams and John Covert, both participants in the First Exhibition of the Society of Independent Artists. Interestingly, *Rongwrong* also includes a table listing the moves of a chess game between Picabia and Roché, which is printed without commentary. It may well be the same game referred to in the Arensberg piece published in *391* no. 7, which would account for the critical letter from "Douxami" that opens the issue (after all, Duchamp was also an editor of *The Blindman*), and Picabia's cryptic response to Douxami and to *tous ceux qui savent*.

The irreverent spirit and satirical humor of *Rongwrong* and *The Blindman* had been foreshadowed by *The Ridgefield Gazook* ("Published unnecessarily whenever the spirit moves us"), a proto-Dada magazine edited by Man Ray, who was then living in an artists' colony in Ridgefield, New Jersey. Its first and only issue ("No. 0") appeared on March 31, 1915. *The Ridgefield Gazook* consisted of a single sheet of paper folded in half twice, with four "pages" of handwritten and drawn material appearing on one side of the paper. The work in question — all of it by the editor — includes a series of parodic texts and images organized in mock sections ("Graftsmanship," "Soshall Science," and "Il'litter-ature"), and attributed to friends who are identified through punning pseudonyms: Adolf Wolff appears as "Adolf Lupo," Alfred Kreymborg as "A. Kreambug," Adon Lacroix (née Donna Lecœur, Man Ray's first wife) as "Adon La†," etc. The cover sports a drawing of two cockroach-like insects copulating, its title "The Cosmic Urge — with ape-ologies to PIcASSo," scrawled underneath.

Man Ray would edit two more magazines before leaving for Paris in 1921. Like *The Ridgefield Gazook*, they, too, lasted but a single issue each. The first of

Rongwrong, first and only issue (1917).

The Ridgefield Gazook, no. 0 (1915); all pages.

these, entitled *TNT*, was published in March 1919. It was the most elaborate of the three periodicals, and was also the most diverse with respect to its contents

Man Ray. TNT. 1919. Cover. Yale Collection of American Literature, Beinecke Rare Book and Manuscript Library, Yale University, New Haven

and contributors. It included writings by Adon Lacroix, Walter Arensberg, and Philippe Soupault (who that same year co-authored the "first Surrealist work" — *Les Champs magnétiques* — with André Breton), among others, and reproductions of artwork by Louis Bouché, Charles Sheeler, and Marcel Duchamp. Man Ray himself was represented by five texts written for collages he had made in 1916–17 (*Revolving Doors*) as well as by an "aerograph" (i.e., a painting made with an airbrush). The cover featured a reproduction of an abstract sculpture by Adolf Wolff. It appeared beneath the title of the magazine, which was printed in large, sans serif letters. Though Man Ray later described *TNT* as a politically radical paper, as Francis Naumann has pointed out, "other than the magazine's explosive title ... there was little in the publication that could be even remotely construed as politically subversive."[7]

In 1921 Man Ray teamed up with Marcel Duchamp to edit what would be the first, indeed the only, American periodical to officially affiliate itself with the Dada movement, which it did with the blessing of Tristan Tzara. Ironically, *New York Dada*, as the publication was called, marked the end of Dada in America. Man Ray later noted the hopelessness of their attempt to attract attention to their activities, "as futile as trying to grow lilies in the desert," he later wrote.[8]

New York Dada ran a total of four pages, and included contributions by many of the usual suspects: a reproduction of one of Duchamp's Readymades graced the cover, and inside there were photographs by Man Ray and Stieglitz, a cartoon by Rube Goldberg, and a long, unsigned poem by Marsden Hartley. There was also a lengthy letter from Tzara himself, a response to Duchamp's request for authorization to use the name "Dada" in the title of their new magazine. "Dada belongs to everybody." Tzara replied, "Like the idea of God or of the toothbrush." The issue also included the spoof of a society-page announcement for a coming-out party to be given by Mina Loy for her protégés: the Marsden Hartleys, and the Joseph Stellas, with music by Edgard Varèse. The issue concluded with two photographs of Dada darling Baroness Elsa von Freytag-Loringhoven (actually stills

---

TNT, first and only issue (1919).

from a film co-produced by Man Ray and Duchamp entitled *Elsa, Baroness von Freytag-Loringhoven, Shaves Her Pubic Hair*), and an announcement that Schwitters would be exhibited — and was, for the first in the States — at the Société Anonyme, Inc.

By the time copies of *New York Dada* hit the streets, Dada in America had all but ceased to exist. The group of friends had dispersed, and many of them left New York for Europe. Picabia was among the first to go, sailing for Switzerland in 1918. He resettled in Paris the following year, as did Gleizes and Roché. By the summer of 1921, both Duchamp and Man Ray were also living in Paris, and de Zayas returned to the French capital that same year. The movement, it seems, was as ephemeral as the publications that promoted it, which is perhaps not coincidental. As Francis Naumann has suggested:

New York Dada, first and only issue (1921).

[The] short-lived existence of this movement in America can actually be looked upon as one of its more positive features. If Dadaism was designed from its inception to be nothing and self-destructive, as many of its proponents claimed, then the movement experienced its most successful manifestation in New York, where in the period of just a few months in the spring of 1921, it died almost before its birth![9]

Notes

[1] de Zayas, p. 184.
[2] As quoted in Naumann, p. 60.
[3] Sanouillet, vol. II, p. 46.
[4] Sanouillet, ibid., p. 47.
[5] Naumann, p. 67.
[6] Sanouillet, vol. II, p. 81.
[7] Naumann, p. 87.
[8] As quoted in Naumann, p. 101.
[9] Naumann, p. 211.

1920–1930 / The Here of There

As George Putnam put it, cosmopolitanism was not seen as a virtue at the end of the 19th and beginning of the 20th centuries. His observation was borne out in a statement printed in the October 1902 issue of *The Dial*, where the author of an article on "Literary Cosmopolitanism" did not hesitate to decry "the occasional aberrations of taste and extravagances of enthusiasm that may accompany the new habit of looking abroad for the fresh inspiration or the fertilizing thought." But since it was easier to travel, and since it could be difficult for young blood to stay at home, more and more people were setting out for distant lands, and staying abroad for longer periods of time. Those who decided to stay where they wound up would write home, describing what they saw/heard/read, and comparing what they remembered of their native land to what they discovered in their adopted home.

Ezra Pound was among the first to leave, initially settling in London, before moving on to Paris a few years later. It was from London that in October 1913 he wrote his first "Letter" for *Poetry*, under the simple title "Paris," in which he recounted his journey through contemporary French literature. From England, he had his eyes set on the Parisian scene, arguing that "If our writers would keep their eyes on Paris instead of on London — the London of today or of yesterday — there might be some chance of their doing work that would not be *démodé* before it gets to the press." According to Pound, American writers could have benefited greatly from a closer reading of French literature: "I think if our American bards would study Remy de Gourmont for rhythm, Laurent Tailhade for delineation, Henri de Régnier for simplicity of syntactical construction, Francis Jammes for humanity, and the faculty of rendering one's own time; and if they would get some idea of intensity from Tristan Corbière (since they will not take their Villon in the original), there might be some hope for American poetry." And because he knew that "the most difficult part of approaching a foreign literature, especially the contemporary foreign literature, consists in finding what books to begin on," he gave a list of "must reads," which included Tristan Corbière, Henri de Régnier, Laurent Tailhade, Remy de Gourmont, Francis Jammes, Arthur Rimbaud, and, among the younger writers, Jules Romains, Charles Vildrac, Henri-Martin Barzun, André Spire (who according to Pound is "something very like an Imagiste"), and Guillaume Apollinaire, whose *Alcools* "is clever."

Pound's message was heard and followed by his compatriots as soon as the circumstances permitted it, which is to say at the end of 1918, when the Armistice was signed, and the First World War over.

Expatriate Magazines

> *Paris is currently more popular than ever as a home*
> *for American intellectuals and artists.*
> — VALERY LARBAUD,
> *"Une renaissance de la poésie américaine"*

Many young poets discovered Europe while fighting on the side of the British and the French. Once the war ended, they went home promising themselves to return at a later, quieter moment and explore things further. Most of them kept their promise, and were back within a few years, transforming Paris into the center of Franco-American activity. American writers saw the French capital as a haven where life was not only cheap but "wet" (there was no prohibition or restriction on alcohol), where freedom applied not only to words but also to behavior, and where people were ready to listen to and read a "new" literature. Hot on the heels of the writers, publishers (who were frequently writers themselves) settled in Paris, and were thus closer to their authors and potential readers. The enforced puritan attitude that characterized the American scene was, to say the least, unwelcoming to this new generation, since publishers in the United States generally refused to print "degenerate" texts by writers like Gertrude Stein or James Joyce. In France not only could those texts be printed without fear of censorship, they would also find readers there. Hence the birth — virtually overnight — of a new breed of publishers, who sometimes went into business for the love of a single work.

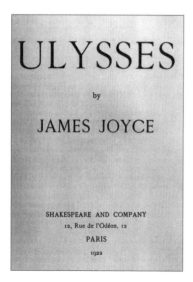

James Joyce's *Ulysses*, Paris, Shakespeare and Company (1922).

Among those, the most well-known is undoubtedly Sylvia Beach, who created an imprint solely to make James Joyce's *Ulysses* available. Though she would publish nothing more, by running her bookstore and lending library she exerted a major influence on the dissemination of Anglophone literature in Europe, as Valery Larbaud stated in the *Revue de France*: "I shall be doing a service in pointing out the most complete and modern Anglo-American library that Paris possesses. It is Shakespeare and Company run by Miss Sylvia Beach whose role as a publisher and propagandist in France of the most recent English and American works assure her from now on an enviable place in the literary history of the United States, and who assembles the elite among

the young English, Irish and Americans who are temporarily in Paris."[1] And, as Sylvia Beach herself wrote in her memoirs, the bookstore became the first Parisian stop for Americans, whether they lived in Paris or were just visiting: "The news of my bookshop, to my surprise, soon spread all over the United States, and it was the first thing the pilgrims looked up in Paris. They were all customers at Shakespeare and Company, which many of them looked upon as their club. ... Every day someone whose work I had seen in *The Little Review* or *The Dial* would appear."[2]

To her club members she offered the latest issues of the New York and Chicago magazines as well as the Paris and London publications, and she received

Sylvia Beach on the doorstep of her bookstore Shakespeare & Company (1931).

regular shipments of books from the other side of the Atlantic. Shakespeare & Co. was thus more than a shop, it was a place where one could keep an eye on what was happening, who was writing, who was published, and who was publishing.

The Dial, The Little Review, and *Poetry* all found their way to the rue de l'Odéon, but more important for the "pilgrims" were those publications printed in Paris representing literary actuality. These magazines were mostly American, both in their intentions and in the language they used; rare indeed were journals that welcomed the idea of literary exchanges, and rarer still were bilingual journals. Most American magazines, whether published in Europe or in the United States, aimed at an Anglophone audience, and most French magazines did not even acknowledge the presence of American writers living in their own community. Magazines on both sides of the Atlantic tended to avoid translation, and when they did present contemporary foreign work, they did so in the original language.

The Exile, Gargoyle, and *The Transatlantic Review* — though based in Paris — either did not or only very rarely published literature in translation. That is not to say they didn't reach a foreign audience, however: many French poets read the above magazines though they were not intended for them, and Americans living in Paris were regular readers of French magazines presenting the latest trends in French literature. If there was no cross publishing to speak of, there was at least some cross reading, which undoubtedly led to cross fertilization. Only a few magazines actively attempted to bridge the two worlds, publishing work in both languages and for both audiences: *Echanges, Tambour,* and to a lesser extent *transition.*

Echanges was edited by Allanah Harper, a young British woman in love with poetry. Published by the Editions Fourcade, *Echanges* was a "Quarterly of English and French Literature" whose goal was to expose Anglophone writers to their French counterparts and vice-versa. The table of contents presented French, British, and American writers in French translation, occasionally with the original *en face.* The few issues that were published included poems by Stephen Hudson (no. 2, 1930) and Norman Douglas (no. 3, June 1930), as well as a text by Louis Zukofsky on the Cantos of Ezra Pound (no. 3, June 1930) and a "Portrait of Picasso" by Gertrude Stein (no. 1, December 1929). *Echanges* was not long-lived,

Echanges, no. 4 (1931).

however. Founded in 1929, it disappeared in 1931, after only a few issues.

When Harold J. Samuelson arrived in Paris, he was not quite eighteen, but he knew very well what he wanted. Born in Chicago in 1910, he had been partly educated in Paris, where his parents had settled in the early '20s. After his father's death in 1927, he decided to invest the money that was supposed to pay for his college education in a literary venture.

The first issue of *Tambour* was published in 1929, and featured André Spire, Ralph Cheever Dunning, Philippe Soupault, Countee Cullen, Blaise Cendrars, Touchagues, Maurice Courtois-Suffit, E. James Olson, Mario Montanard, Liang-Tsong-Tai, Stuart Gilbert, and Harold J. Samuelson himself. This eclectic line-up not only reflected Samuelson's personality, but also revealed his ideas on literature and the arts. The founder of *Tambour* never considered himself an expatriate, "but rather a bilingual writer who had been raised in both French and American cultures," an attitude evident throughout the magazine: texts in *Tambour* were not systematically translated, but sometimes appeared in the original language. For publicity purposes, he defined his magazine as "An international review of literature and the arts, publishing American, French and English writers in the original." He did not want his magazine to be the voice of a movement, but a forum for all existing trends in both cultures, unifying them under the banner of "progress," as his motto suggests: "To interpret the past is to express the present; to express the present is to create the future." Thanks to its bilingual format, *Tambour* was informed by both periodical traditions: inspired by the Anglophone model, it devoted large sections to innovative poetry, and, following French models, it also featured reviews and notes on art, literature, music (even phonograph records), theater, and film, which was one of the passions of the editor.

There were two special issues: issue 5, dedicated to Anatole France, who had died in 1924, and issue 7, which included contributions by eleven Italian poets (whose work was translated into French, but not English). When *Tambour* disappeared after its eighth issue ("Little reviews, like public conveyances, are sometimes obliged to stop"), the only real binational magazine disappeared.

Founded by Eugene Jolas in 1927, *transition* published French and Anglophone artists and writers for twelve years. At first a monthly, *transition* began appearing quarterly in 1928, then sporadically in 1929–1930, when it experienced financial difficulties and had to cease publication until 1932. At that point Jolas was able to gather funds allowing one or two hefty issues a year.

transition appeared in English and was aimed primarily at an Anglophone audience, though the ambition of the editors — Jolas, his wife Maria, and Elliot Paul, who was soon replaced by Robert Sage — was to produce "An International Quarterly for Creative Experiment." Wishing "to present the quintessence of the modern spirit in evolution," Jolas diligently published James Joyce's "Work in

Progress" (the working title for *Finnegans Wake*), which formed the core of the magazine. This helped define *transition*, which soon became a touchstone for creative and experimental literature.

The scope of the magazine was American and European, but most of the writers published were either Americans living in Paris or French. Among the latter were Surrealists Paul Eluard, Robert Desnos, and Philippe Soupault; work by Tristan Tzara was also included. In the end, the French contribution to *transition* was minimal, and *transition*'s pages were dominated by the expatriates and occasional homebodies like William Carlos Williams. According to Philippe Soupault himself, though *transition* served as the voice of the expatriate poets, it was an invaluable asset to the evolution of French poetry: "At a time when we stood in France before the collapse of all poetic values, when those most qualified to consider poetry had become discouraged, and when, for reasons that seem to me superfluous to enumerate here, those same persons turned their attention in other directions, *transition* represented the only living force, the only review which did not despair of poetry, and thus authorized the poets to continue their work." (*transition* in France — June 1930).

As is evident in his editing of *transition*, Jolas was committed to bringing innovative American poetry to the French public. Thus, when his friend and contributor to the magazine, Philippe Soupault, asked him to put together an anthology of new American poetry, he enthusiastically took up the task, producing in 1928 the groundbreaking *Anthologie de la Nouvelle Poésie Américaine*. His goal was to reflect on the poetic spirit of pre- and postwar America, showing the "obvious" (to his eyes) difference between the new generation and the preceding one. To compile his anthology, Jolas relied not only on his own knowledge, but also on another work, the *Modern*

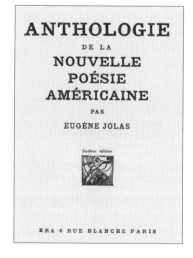

top: *transition*, no. 24 (1936).
bottom: Eugene Jolas' *Anthologie de la Nouvelle Poésie Américaine*, Paris (1928).

American Poetry published in a "revised and enlarged edition" by the poet Louis Untermeyer by Harcourt, Brace & Co. in 1921. His selection thus reflected the dif-
ferent "schools" and movements active in the United States since the 1912 Renaissance, as well as the Paris expatriates. His choice was voluntarily inclusive, "for documentary reasons," as he explained in his foreword, where he had this to say about the then state of American poetry:

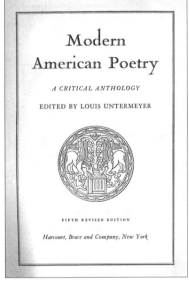

> Though I recognize that this poetry is endowed with a variety and a wealth of experience rare among contemporary European poets, I must say that in general, the originality of modern American poetry stems from purely external effects. It will have to go beyond the materialistic stage and attain a contemplation and inspiration liberated from an essentially dynamic civilization, in order to possess the spirit that we all wish for this young nation.

While *Echanges*, *Tambour*, and *transition* pub-
lished writers working in both languages, most Paris-based Anglophone magazines did not. At best, they ran an occasional French poem, or dedicated a special issue to French literature, just as any magazine printed outside of Paris could have done. Such was the case with *This Quarter*, whose editors acknowledged the influence of their French surroundings, but printed mostly Anglophone poets.

This Quarter was founded in 1925 by Ethel Moorhead, a Scot, and the American Ernest Walsh. Its first issue was dedicated to Ezra Pound who, in the words of its editors, "by his creative work, his editorship of several magazines, his helpful friendship for young and unknown artists, his many and untiring efforts to win better appreciation of what is first rate in art comes first to our mind as meriting the gratitude of this generation." As the special Pound issue suggests, the magazine was particularly open to creative and innovative writing, and published mostly American writers living in Paris. Due to the sudden death of Walsh in 1927, Ethel Moorhead had to interrupt publication while she scrambled to gather enough funding to keep the magazine alive. Unable to do so, she sold the title in 1929, as she announced in the fourth and last issue she was to edit: "I am glad to announce that *This Quarter* has been taken over, and will be carried on, by Mr. Edward W. Titus, the well-known Paris publisher."

Louis Untermeyer's *Modern American Poetry*, New York (1921).

Edward Titus had founded his Black Manikin Press in 1926, having settled in the rue Delambre in Montparnasse, where he had opened the bookstore "At the Sign of Black Manikin" in 1924. Judging from Moorhead's wish that "young writers of worth shall still find [in *This Quarter*] a place for their work," Titus was indeed the right man. As a publisher, he had the reputation of accepting works by unknown authors. The first thing he did as editor of *This Quarter* was ask friends and colleagues to send him "young meritorious writers who find it difficult to get their work published." Not only was Titus true to his word when it came to American and English writers, for the penultimate issue of the magazine he also welcomed the most controversial Surrealists, turning to André Breton, who was invited to edit this "Surrealist Number" (v. 1 [Sept. 1932]). It contained poetry by Breton, Paul Eluard, Benjamin Péret, Tristan Tzara, and Salvador Dalí, as well as the scenario of Dalí and Luis Buñuel's *An Andalusian Dog*, unpublished notes by Duchamp, essays about the movement by Breton, Eluard, Dalí, René Crevel, and Max Ernst, and, to illustrate the issue, works by Giorgio de Chirico, Max Ernst, Valentine Hugo, Man Ray, and Yves Tanguy. The translations were done by Richard Thomas and Samuel Beckett, "the latter earning Titus' 'special acknowledgement,' particularly for his rendering of Eluard's and Breton's poems 'characterizable only in superlatives.' "[3]

This special issue notwithstanding, French literature was not the main concern of the editor, and it was mostly through the commentaries of Harold J. Salemson and of translator Victor Llona that Anglophone readers had a sense of what was going on in France. But despite its rare incursions into French culture, *This Quarter* was essential to Parisian literary life of the time, especially during those years when Eugene Jolas interrupted publication of *transition*, leaving Anglophone readers without other sources for new writing. The magazine disappeared in 1932, when Edward Titus decided to stop all his Parisian publishing ventures, including his press, Black Manikin.

After the first expatriate magazine — *Gargoyle* — was printed in 1921, a number of Anglophone journals suddenly sprang up in Paris, a total of fifteen appearing between 1921 and 1930. Most of them were short-lived — *Gargoyle* itself lasted but a year — but all were motivated by the same sense of enthusiasm and the desire to give voice to their time. Their editors were not only American, but British as well, like Allanah Harper, for example, or Ford Madox Ford who moved to Paris in 1922 to join the American colony, and be closer to those he admired. In January 1924, he founded a literary magazine, *The Transatlantic Review*, for which he asked contributions from Joyce, E.E. Cummings, and Basil Bunting, among others. One year later, he ran out of funds and was forced to close shop. In 1927, Ezra Pound himself put out the first issue of his magazine, *The*

AUGUST · PARIS 1921
GARGOYLE
FIVE FRANCS
NUMBER TWO

Exile, when he felt he could no longer trust American editors to publish "his" authors.

Pound had a special relationship with many American magazines. In order to understand the pivotal role he played in publishing in both the old and the new world, we need to backtrack a bit, and consider a number of magazines published in America in the 1910s.

Gargoyle, no. 2 (1921).

American Magazines

For almost two decades Pound had been the official European correspondent for most American literary magazines. He offered his services to many editors, arguing that living in England gave him a privileged view of what was happening on the Continent. He would send home the cream of his "crop" of European writers, and even contribute his own verse and criticism.

Pound's first contribution came in 1912 to the new *Poetry: A Magazine of Verse*, founded by Harriet Monroe in Chicago, in reaction to the situation of poetry in her country. As she stated in April 1912, in the circular letter in which she presented her project for a new magazine, most publishers would not even consider publishing books of poetry. Magazine editors were no better: "Editors of our most literary magazines state in writing that they cannot publish a poem of more than twenty or thirty lines, 'no matter how meritorious,' 'more than once in a long time.' Some of them say never, under any circumstances. And most editors are forced to accept verse from the standpoint of popularity rather than excellence." And the future editor concluded her account of the situation with this surprising statement: "In short, the vast English-speaking world says to its poets; 'Silence.'" These conclusions moved her to found a new magazine devoted entirely to poetry, entitled simply *Poetry: A Magazine of Verse*, which she described in the first issue, dated October 1912, "as a modest effort to give to poetry her own place, her own voice. The popular magazines can afford her but scant courtesy — a Cinderella corner in the ashes — because they seek a large public which is not hers. ... We believe that there is a public for poetry." And there were certainly poets.

The first issues of *Poetry* marked the beginning of the American Renaissance, the birth of a "new" poetry, as it presented some of the "new" poets: Vachel Lindsay, Ezra Pound (no. 1), Amy Lowell, Carl Sandburg, Robert Frost, and T.S. Eliot, who were soon followed by Marianne Moore, Wallace Stevens, H.D., William Carlos Williams, Robert McAlmon.

In the second issue Harriet Monroe published the "policy of the magazine." She refused to belong to any party, movement, or school, and made a point of keeping an "open door": "may the great poet we are looking for never find it shut, or half-shut, against his ample genius! To this end the editors hope to keep free of entangling alliances with any single class or school. They desire to print the best English verse which is being written today, regardless of where, by whom, or under what theory of art it is written."

And "English verse" was the priority. Just like the magazines that appeared over the following years, *Poetry* lacked an international vision; their goal was to publish American poetry, and show potential readers that it existed and was worth reading.

But Ezra Pound, though attracted by the smell of fresh ink and always looking for an outlet for his own work, did not share this monolingual view. Having promised Monroe exclusivity for his own poetry, he offered his services as a scout for "good" poets, boasting of his ability to "keep the magazine in touch with whatever is most dynamic in artistic thought, either here [in London] or in Paris, as much of it comes to me, and I do see nearly everyone that matters."[4] Pound was true to his word, but his regular shipments consisted almost entirely of Anglophone poetry, and few French poets were ever included. Thus *Poetry* was generally weak in "international" literature, with only an occasional foreign-language poem printed, at times without any English translation. Such was the case of the July 1913 issue, which included Charles Vildrac's "Gloire," and the January 1915 issue, which contained some of Remy de Gourmont's "Epigrammes," Vildrac and Gourmont both being poets that Pound worshiped.

Though very few foreign poets were welcome on the pages of *Poetry* in the early years, its critics and readers were nevertheless interested in the Old World, and many reviews and articles published in *Poetry* focused on literary life on the other side of the Atlantic.

The above remarks also apply to the early years of *The Little Review*. Founded in Chicago in 1914 by Margaret C. Anderson, the journal presented itself as "A Magazine of the Arts, Making No Compromise with the Public Taste," and was open to literature and art, as well as criticism. Soon after its first issue, artist Jane Heap joined Anderson as an associate editor, offering her expertise in both art and criticism. By 1918, Chicago seemed too far from the literary scene they longed for, and the two editors moved the magazine to New York, where all of those who had not left for Europe were living.

During the early years, Heap and Anderson found it difficult to find enough "good" material to fill the sixty-four pages of their magazine. Unlike Harriet Monroe, they had doubts about the quality of then contemporary poetry, and were desperately looking for "good literature." In 1915 they actually issue in which half of the pages were blank, their response to the

A COLLECTION OF WORK BY SOME YOUNG AMERICANS — IN CONTRAST WITH THE WORK OF SOME YOUNG EUROPEANS : MOSTLY FRENCH—SURREALISTE

ERNEST HEMINGWAY
EDWARD NAGLE
MATTHEW JOSEPHSON
MALCOLM COWLEY
JOHN BROOKS WHEELWRIGHT
GORHAM B. MUNSON
SLATER BROWN
CHARLES L. DURBORAW
HART CRANE
JOHN RIORDAN
WILLIAM CARLOS WILLIAMS
GEORGES LIMBOUR

IN THIS NUMBER

EMILE MALESPINE
MICHEL LEIRIS
MARCEL ARLAND
ANDRÉ HARLAIRE
ANDRÉ DESSOR
MARX LOEBE
JOSEPH DELTEIL
JACQUES VIOT
HANS ARP
RENÉ CREVEL
JACQUES BARON
TRISTAN TZARA
G. RIBEMONT DESSAIGNES

REPRODUCTIONS OF PAINTINGS—CONSTRUCTIONS—PHOTOGRAPHY.

the little REVIEW

SPRING–1926–SUMMER

The Little Review, vol. 12, no. 1 (1926).

mediocre submissions they had received. So when Ezra Pound proposed a collaboration, the two editors gratefully accepted the offer: he would be the "European Correspondent" for the magazine, promising again to scout out the finest writing on the other side of the Atlantic. Thus in March 1918, *The Little Review* became the first American magazine to publish James Joyce. Shortly thereafter, American censors forbade the publication of any work by the Irish writer and the editors of *The Little Review* had to abandon their idea of printing installments of *Ulysses* as it was being written. Instead the editors ran Helen Rootham's translation of Rimbaud's *Illuminations*, making those seminal texts available to American readers

---

The Little Review: Exiles' Number, vol. 19, no. 3 (1923).

in English. In the spring of 1923, Heap and Anderson produced a special issue, the "Exile's Number," dedicated to the Paris expatriates. It featured work by Gertrude Stein, Mina Loy, George Antheil, E.E. Cummings, H.D., Robert McAlmon, and Dorothy Shakespear, and sported a cover designed by the painter Fernand Léger. In the fall of the following year, a special issue featured essays and writings on the art of Juan Gris. And in the spring of 1926, an issue entitled "Young Americans" offered its readers "a collection of work by some young Americans, in contrast with the work of some young Europeans: mostly French-Surrealiste."

When the last number of *The Little Review* was printed in 1929, it had dedicated more pages to writers living on the Continent than in America, and was thus one of the major bridges between the two cultures, thanks in great part to the efforts of Pound, whose influence would be felt in another notable American periodical, *The Dial*.

When Scofield Thayer, a young Harvard graduate, bought *The Dial* in 1920, he created a revolution, transforming this long-lived conservative publication into one of the leading journals of contemporary art.

Founded in 1840 and directed by Margaret Fuller, and later Ralph Waldo Emerson, the first *Dial* was a transcendentalist quarterly, printed in Boston. After a first — and very short — resurrection in Cincinnati in 1860, the title was revived in Chicago in 1880 by Francis Browne. At that point, the bi-monthly magazine was considered a midwestern political and social publication. When purchased in 1916 by Martyn Johnson (Browne had died in 1913), it became more of a weekly of radical opinion. But Johnson had to face hard times and was happy to find Thayer and his money.

The emphasis once again was on Anglophone writing, but the editors flattered themselves on being open to international literature and art, so as early as 1920, *The Dial* began featuring work by French writers. French artists were also well represented (as were non-French artists living in France), and readers regularly saw reproductions of work by André Derain, Pablo Picasso, Henri Matisse, Robert Delaunay, or Constantin Brancusi on its pages. Prose had its spokesman: Anatole France, who was, according to the editors, "the greatest of contemporary French writers";

THE

DIAL

APRIL 1922

Dante *Sculpture*	*Alfeo Faggi*	
The Dark City	*Conrad Aiken*	345
Poem	*E. E. Cummings*	354
Chinese Civilization and the West	*Bertrand Russell*	356
An Etching	*Henri-Matisse*	
The Beguine Symforosa	*Felix Timmermans*	365
Donald Evans	*Witter Bynner*	384
Two Drawings *Pen and Ink*	*Sidney D. Carlyle*	
George Sand	*Benedetto Croce*	385
A Line Drawing	*Edward P. Nagle*	
Napoleon	*John Gould Fletcher*	393
Portrait of An Arrived Critic	*Kenneth Burke*	398
Three Pieces of Sculpture	*Wilhelm Lehmbruck*	
Paris Letter	*Ezra Pound*	401
Prague Letter	*Edward Moore*	406
Book Reviews :		
The Perfect Tory	*Robert Morss Lovett*	412
Memoirs of a Midget	*Padraic Colum*	416
This Side of Innocence	*Vivian Shaw*	419
A Child's History of the World	*Charles K. Trueblood*	422
The Best Butter	*Gilbert Seldes*	427
Briefer Mention		431
Modern Art	*Henry McBride*	436
Musical Chronicle	*Paul Rosenfeld*	439
The Theatre	*G. S.*	444
Comment	*The Editors*	446

VOLUME LXXII NUMBER 4

50 cents a copy

The Dial, vol. LXXII, no. 4 (1922).

in 1921, they proudly published *La Vie en Fleur* simultaneously with the French edition. Though not the main priority, poetry was not forgotten; it had been present from the beginning, but in limited quantities, generally one or two poems per issue. In 1920, the poetry of Charles Cros and Arthur Rimbaud was featured, and in 1921, *The Dial*'s readers discovered Charles Vildrac and André Spire, along with Paul Valéry, Remy de Gourmont, and Paul Morand. The latter actually alternated writing the "Letter from Paris" with the inevitable Ezra Pound, who yet again assumed the role of the "Foreign correspondent." Due to his influence, writers that had been published in *The Little Review* and *Poetry* also appeared in *The Dial*, the latter being the latest outlet for Pound's discoveries as well as for his own work.

Despite the relative success of the magazine, Scofield Thayer decided to resign in June 1926 and Marianne Moore became the editor until the last issue in July 1929.

French Magazines

It takes a particular kind of person, not to mention a fair amount of dedication, to play the part of the *passeur* or "go-between." In the literary world the role implies certain qualities: a commitment to a particular kind of literature, a desire to communicate one's passion, and, in some cases, a commitment to translation. The *passeur*'s name appears at the bottom of translated texts, after the last line of a *chronique*, or as the guest editor of a special section or issue of a magazine. He is the one to whom editors turn when they need to beef up their pages with some translations, the one queried for his expertise in this or that area, and, too often, the one forgotten by literary history, since he is perceived as being but a transmitter — not a creator — of literature.

This, of course, is a fallacy. Many *passeurs* had a literary life of their own, while others "just" wrote articles and translated. And limiting our discussion to translators would leave out all those who did not translate but championed "their" writers in other ways. Valery Larbaud and Jean Catel were two of the most prominent *passeurs* in Paris, both for what they wrote and for the influence they exerted on editors.

Valery Larbaud declared himself an "Anglicist" in 1901, when he proposed his first article to the editor of *La Plume*, a Symbolist magazine that was open to young critics and welcomed translations. After they ran his essay on "Celtic songs," Larbaud offered to write an article on "recent poetry in the United States." He named three poets: Whittier, James Russell Lowell, and Walt Whitman, but the article never materialized; at the time Larbaud was more interested in the Lake District Poets and Walter Savage Landor than in their American counterparts,

Whitman excepted, of course. Nevertheless, in Spetember 1921 he sent the *Revue de France* a long article on the "Renaissance de la poésie américaine," which appeared over two issues. His reflection on the rebirth of American poetry is — like Jolas' — based on the new edition of Louis Untermeyer's anthology, *Modern American Poetry*. Following Untermeyer's example, he split his article into three sections: the Chicago School, the Boston School, and the New York School. The first one, the Chicago School, is best represented in his mind by Vachel Lindsay, on whom he had already written an essay the year before. According to Larbaud, Amy Lowell and Robert Frost embodied the spirit of the Boston School, whereas the poets of the New York School were "the most recent, the newest, and the freest of 19th century influences" and their official magazine was *The Dial*, published in the city by Scofield Thayer.

This article, along with Jean Catel's *chroniques*, which appeared in *Les Marges* and *Mercure de France*, helped French readers understand where American poetry was going. But Larbaud won his place in the French-American pantheon of critics when he wrote an article on William Carlos Williams, a poet he admired — and the feeling was mutual — and considered one of the most original of his generation.

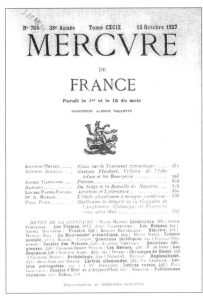

Unlike Larbaud, Jean Catel actually visited the United States before ever writing anything about America. "Invalided by the war, he was sent to the United States by the French Government to aid in that general rapprochement so much desired in this cosmopolitan day," as Henry Blake Fuller wrote in an article on Catel that was published in the March 1920 issue of *Poetry*. To fulfill his mission, Catel spent a year at the University of Minnesota, studying the American poets of his day and presenting his observations in a paper entitled "The American Image." According to Fuller, the French poet and student wished to "understand better the wonderland which had given birth to Whitman and Poe." And, according to articles later published in French magazines, not only did he come to understand that world, he also found a new wave of poets making "an admirable attempt at creating the traditional background that sustains art." In his dissertation, he wrote of the importance and influence of Walt Whitman on modern French and American poetry, and gave regular lectures on modern poets at the University of Grenoble. While still a student, Catel contributed

Mercure de France, vol. CXCIX, no. 704 (1927).

many *chroniques* and articles to *Mercure de France*, where he was the official "correspondent" for American literature.

Though Larbaud and Catel kept an eye on what was happening on the American poetry scene, their efforts were not reflected in the pages of French literary magazines, since in the 1920s prose was the dominant force. As French readers became acquainted with Ernest Hemingway, John Dos Passos, F. Scott Fitzgerald, William Faulkner, and Sherwood Anderson, poetry was increasingly marginalized. Rare indeed were those magazines that were open to Anglophone poets, and fewer still were interested in contemporary writing, which led to a paradox: though a good deal of innovative American poetry was then being written in Paris, it was not being printed in the French magazines published there. Part of the explanation, as we have already seen with the American expatriate magazines, is that the two communities did not really mix, and when they did they tended to communicate in one or the other of the two languages, and did not feel compelled to translate. This situation was reflected by the trajectory of writers and readers in the Rue de l'Odéon, as they crossed from one side of the street to the other, leaving the Maison des Amis des Livres to browse in Shakespeare and Company.

Located on the east side of the street, the Maison des Amis des Livres, the Francophone counterpart of Shakespeare and Company, was, according to Larbaud, "indisputably the founder of the present bookshop movement. It introduced two great principles which have now been established: the first, of a moral order, demands that the bookseller be not only cultivated but that he or she undertake the task of a veritable priesthood; the second, of a material order, reposes on the practice of the sale and loan of books. The Library of the Maison des Amis des Livres is today the most complete and the richest library in existence. It possesses a great number of works that are out of print. There one finds all the moderns up to the most extreme, and all the Classics." A lending library and a bookstore, the Maison des Amis des Livres was also the center of a very active intellectual life, which included regular exhibits and conferences. It was there that in 1922, on May 31, Paul Valéry agreed for the first time to talk in front of an audience, to introduce his peers to the "Ideas of Edgar Poe."

The shelves of the bookstore were covered not only with books, but also with numerous magazines, from the first issues of *Vers et Prose* up to the most recent issues of magazines founded and run by young and unknown but courageous writers and literary activists. And sometimes, Adrienne Monnier did more than just present those items on her shelves: she offered to administrate and distribute many of those magazines, such as *Intentions, Commerce,* and later, in the 1930s, *Mesures. Intentions* never really published any American poets, and *Commerce* published only a few. Founded in 1924 by Marguerite Caetani, Princess of Bassiano, it was a luxurious magazine, whose editors were no less than Valery

Larbaud, Paul Valéry, and Léon-Paul Fargue. It was meant to be a publication of international literature, prose and poetry, and had no real program, other than a demand for quality. During its eight-year existence, several American writers were

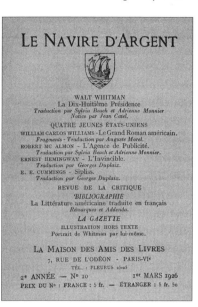

published in *Commerce*, but few of them were poets: the notes of Edgar Allan Poe, in a translation by Paul Valéry, and poems by Archibald MacLeish, translated by Larbaud.

In 1925, Adrienne Monnier founded her own magazine, *Le Navire d'Argent*, but despite her ties to Sylvia Beach and the American community in Paris, she would not publish any American writers before the tenth issue. In March 1926, under the title "Quatre jeunes États-Uniens," Sylvia Beach presented prose works by four young Americans: William Carlos Williams, Robert McAlmon, Ernest Hemingway, and E.E. Cummings. The number was introduced by a translation of Walt Whitman's "18th Presidentiad," translated by Adrienne Monnier and Sylvia Beach themselves.

Though most magazines did not print much poetry, they did talk about it, especially in the "Letters from ...," a feature in favor with editors and readers at the time. Supposedly sent from abroad, these "Letters" contained descriptions of the social, political, and/or literary state of a given country. The form allowed a certain freedom with respect to topics covered, and the chronicler was not required to paint a detailed portrait of the situation — a snapshot of matters important, interesting, or simply notable, would suffice. Jean Catel signed a few such letters in *Mercure de France*, while Upton Sinclair and Pearl Buck sent a "Lettre des États-Unis," and Gorham B. Munson a "Chronique américaine," to *Europe*. Several of these letters appeared alongside various *chroniques* and reviews in the *Revue Européenne*, a magazine founded in 1916 by André Germain, a lover of literature. The *Revue Européenne* began a new life when Germain asked Valery Larbaud, Edmond Jaloux, and Philippe Soupault to edit it in 1922. Larbaud and Jaloux represented an

top: *Le Navire d'Argent*, no. 10 (1926).
bottom: *La Revue Européenne*, no. 35 (1926).

older generation, but were both committed to translation and European literature, an ideal that the young Soupault found easy to endorse. As Soupault himself had

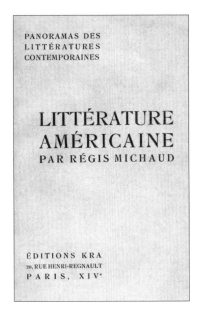

PANORAMAS DES
LITTÉRATURES
CONTEMPORAINES

LITTÉRATURE
AMÉRICAINE
PAR RÉGIS MICHAUD

ÉDITIONS KRA
20, RUE HENRI-REGNAULT
PARIS, XIVᵉ

many friends in the expatriate community, the young editor presented a number of American writers in the magazine, publishing substantial selections of writing by Sherwood Anderson, F. Scott Fitzgerald, and Carl Van Vechten. When Germain gave editorial direction to the three writers, he also asked publisher Simon Kra to take over the management of the magazine, keeping for himself the role of *mécène*. The chief advantage of this association with Kra was to be able to pursue the editorial strategy developed with the magazine in the form of book publications. Under the banner Kra/Sagittaire, many titles were published, but no Anglophone poetry, however, except for Jolas' *Anthologie de la Nouvelle Poésie Américaine* and ten pages dedicated to the "New poetry" in Régis Michaud's *Littérature Américaine*.

Directly inspired by *Commerce* and the *Revue Européenne*, *Bifur* was intended to be international in scope, and open to all arts (the magazine frequently featured reproductions of photographs and paintings), as well as to political trends. According to its editors, Italian journalist Nino Franck and former Dadaist Georges Ribemont-Dessaignes, there were no geographical or "racial" limits imposed. They enlisted six "foreign" correspondents: James Joyce, Boris Pilniak, William Carlos Williams, Bruno Barilli, Ramon Gomez de la Serna, and Gottfried Benn, all of whom were to solicit work from the best writers in their respective countries. Williams was one of the most active, providing the editors with many contacts, two of which actually materialized: Jean Toomer and Langston Hughes. Toomer wrote a "Lettre d'Amérique" for the first issue, commenting on the personality of the newly elected president, Herbert Hoover, while in the second issue William Carlos Williams himself

BIFUR

8

ÉDITIONS DU CARREFOUR
BOULEVARD SAINT-GERMAIN, 160, PARIS, VIᵉ

expressed his feelings on some of Hoover's policies. For his part, Harold J. Salemson, an old friend of Franck, denounced prohibition, arguing that it actually

top: Regis Michaud's *Littérature américaine*, Paris (1926).
bottom: *Bifur*, no. 8 (1931).

harmed the people it was supposed to protect. The last American contribution was a chapter of a novel in progress by Langston Hughes. All of this writing, both fiction and nonfiction, dealt with the political and social situation of the United States in the late 1920s, introducing French readers to themes and issues that would dominate the following decade. By the time *Bifur* published its first issue in 1929, the golden years had passed, and many American publishers and writers returned to the United States, out of funds and unprepared to face the Depression.

Notes

[1]This statement was run as an ad — in English — for La Maison des amis des livres.

[2]Beach, p. 23.

[3]Ford, 1975, p. 166.

[4]Letter from Ezra Pound to Harriet Monroe, dated August 18, 1912, as quoted in Williams, p. 15.

1930–1950 / There and Back

Oh we do not realize what France means to the world!
Especially to this world whose end we think we see —
and see nothing clear — nothing but change without
reference to THINGS, of which the world is made.
— WILLIAM CARLOS WILLIAMS,
"The Genius of France"

B Y 1931 MOST OF THE EXPATRIATES had returned home, where they struggled to make a living while waiting for better times. Many worried about the changing political climate in Europe, and were anxious about the sinking economy in their own country. Money had become scarce and was spent only on the essential, which was also the case in Europe, for the effects of the Depression were felt on both continents.

In such a context, literary magazines were not "essential," and the play money traditionally used to fund them had vanished. In France only those magazines with institutional backing or sources of private funding survived: *transition* would be published until 1938, and institutions like the *Nouvelle Revue Française* and *Mercure de France* carried on well beyond that. The situation was similar in the United States, where certain magazines had endured the Crash: the indestructible *North American Review*, the *Southern Review*, and the *American Mercury* or *Scribner's Magazine*, which ran until 1939. In both countries, however, magazine activity slowed considerably, and the few new literary periodicals that appeared at the time tended to be socially motivated and political in tone.

In France

Created in 1923, *Europe* was a model for "committed" literary magazines. Its political leanings are evident in the selections chosen by the editors, who favored writers with a cause. In the fall of 1930, Paul Nizan presented French readers with work by American "proletarian poets," and poems by Langston Hughes were repeatedly printed, appearing in 1932, 1937, 1949, and 1950. The *chronique* devoted to the United States usually dealt with the economical and social situation in that country, and literature itself was rarely mentioned. In October 1934, for example, François Crucy's "Chronique du temps: Californie" focused on a strike that had taken place in San Francisco the previous spring, detailing the issues at stake, and describing the negotiations between the strikers and the

Chamber of Commerce of the city. In April 1937, Jean-Richard Bloch recalled how Caron de Beaumarchais, the famous playwright, had also supported American Independence, siding with the Americans and gathering money and arms to be sent overseas. In writing about this event, Bloch sought to remind the French of their previous commitments to freedom and democracy, drawing parallels between the situation in the former British colony and the Spanish civil war. On those occasions when American literature was presented, the focus was on committed writers such as John Steinbeck or John Dos Passos. Philippe Soupault wrote a long article on Dos Passos in 1934, when most of his works were translated.

Having resigned from his position at the *Revue Européenne*, Soupault became a journalist, and was thus able to fulfill his dream: traveling to the United States, which he did on assignment for *Paris-Soir*. His task was a simple one: to write about what he saw. Throughout his stay in the United States, Soupault sent articles and reviews back to French literary magazines, giving accounts of books he read and relating his discoveries. In October 1934 he contributed a major text to *Europe* — "La nouvelle littérature américaine" — in which he tried to assess the current state of American poetry. In doing so, he also drew conclusions on the expatriate experience of the '20s:

> The important rapprochement of nascent American "avant-garde" writers and French "schools" must not be underestimated, neither from the critical nor the aesthetic point of view. Strictly speaking, there has been no real, profound influence. Rather, a commonality of views has confirmed young American writers in their tendencies and practices. It should be noted that this fraternization emphasized the "radical" character of certain works and helped certain minds mature and realize their true orientation.

Now back at home, Soupault argued, the expatriates have rediscovered their country, and have found a new voice:

> This new American poetry is still difficult to define, because it is still being created. It is attempting to discover, to recognize itself. The poets themselves seem to be awakening from a dream. Eyes closed, they are moving toward the spot where one day (no one can say when) they will deposit their common treasures.

Europe, no. 134 (1934).

The poets Soupault had in mind when he wrote these lines included Robert Frost, Vachel Lindsay, Carl Sandburg, William Carlos Williams, and Robinson Jeffers, but also Jean Toomer, Claude McKay, and Countee Cullen.

Toomer, McKay, Cullen, and Hughes had also crossed the Atlantic in the '20s, in search of a life free from racial oppression. In France they found a haven where they could live as they chose, and where publishing opportunities were not determined by skin color. While Europe was hardly free of prejudice, there was no systematic repression in Paris, and that fact, coupled with the popularity enjoyed by African American artists in the French capital, made these writers feel that they could participate fully in literary life there. Coincidentally, in France at the time, magazines were springing up to defend and promote *Négritude*, to champion the cause of people of African descent, and to fight colonization. The most famous of these publications was *La Revue du Monde Noir / The Review of the Black World*, founded by Paulette and Andrée Nardal, two sisters from the French Antilles who came to Paris to complete their education and eventually settled there. Their house was a meeting place for Antilleans living in the metropolitan area, and, as a result of their many meetings and discussions, they decided to publish a magazine that would reflect their views and promote black writing the world over. Their ambition was to be read wherever there were readers, specifically, black readers. Thus, *La Revue du Monde Noir* was published in both French and in English, and lasted six issues, from the fall of 1931 to the end of 1932. The Nardal sisters wished to give voice to the richness of black cultures from around the world, and intended their magazine to spread ideas of freedom and unity within the international Black community, as stated in the first issue:

> Our Aim:
> To give to the intelligentsia of the black race and their partisans an official organ in which to publish their artistic, literary and scientific works.
> To study and to popularize, by means of the press, books, lectures, courses, all which concerns Negro Civilization and the natural riches of Africa, thrice sacred to the black race.
> The triple aim which *La Review du Monde Noir* [sic] will pursue, will be: to create among the Negroes of the entire world, regardless of nationality, an intellectual, and moral tie, which will permit them to better know each other, to love one another, to defend more effectively their collective interests and to glorify their race.

The Nardal sisters published poems by Langston Hughes and Claude McKay in the third issue of *La Revue du Monde Noir*, Hughes's contribution being "I, Too," in which, recalling Whitman, he writes: "I, too, sing America/.../ I, too, am America."

In a society that was becoming more politicized each day, there were still some editors who eschewed social relevance and published writers not for their political ideologies, but for the literary qualities of their works. Eugene Jolas, for example, never varied his editorial line after he put out the first issue of *transition*. There was even the occasional newcomer who dreamed of producing a luxurious magazine dedicated fully to literature. Such was the case with Henry Church, editor of *Mesures*.

The first issue of *Mesures* was published in Paris in 1935. Its editorial board was prestigious and cosmopolitan: gathered around founder Henry Church, "a

French-speaking American writer"[1] who invested part of his fortune in the magazine, were philosopher Bernhard Groethuysen, poet Henri Michaux, Jean Paulhan, who was director of the *Nouvelle Revue Française*, and Italian poet Giuseppe Ungaretti. And of course, at the heart of this project were the two booksellers from the rue de l'Odéon: Adrienne Monnier and Sylvia Beach. At Paulhan's request, Monnier agreed to manage the magazine, a task that "did not please [her] very much" as it consisted of "bookkeeping, management, business correspondence." She resigned in 1937, and the position was filled by publisher José Corti. On the other side of the street, Sylvia Beach was also put to work: she was to assist the board in contacting Anglophone writers, and in finding suitable translators for them.

The goal of Henry Church and his editorial board was to publish, "irrespective of any fashion, school, or doctrine, work by the best French or foreign writers, as well as philosophical, mystical, and ancient texts." Poets and writers published in *Mesures* include Auden, Isherwood, Forster, Edgar Lee Masters, Frost, Powys, Joyce, and Gerard Manley Hopkins, as well as Henri Michaux, Jean Prévost, Jean Paulhan, and other writers of the *Nouvelle Revue Française*. Even though it was mostly a Franco-American collaboration, *Mesures* was not a Franco-American magazine; it was meant to be a literary window on the world, and it featured work by Russian, Italian, Spanish, German, Indian, and Chinese writers, in addition to their French and American counterparts.

In 1939, the editorial board decided to dedicate an issue to American literature. Cautiously, however, they warned their readers:

Mesures, no. 3 (1939).

Note:

      The reader should not expect a faithful, complete representation of American literature on the pages that follow. Some writers were dropped because they were too well known, others because we had already published them or because the translation was bad. Though incomplete, the present collection is vibrant, worthy of interest and astonishing, on many accounts. If it didn't sound slightly pretentious, we might have called this issue an American source book.

An American source book? The eclectic table of contents seems to illustrate this ambition: the issue opens with a letter written by an 18th-century French missionary, which is followed by Cotton Mather's retelling of the Salem witch trials, after which comes a letter from Benjamin Franklin to "those who wish to emigrate," another letter from John Paul Jones to Franklin, a text by French immigrant Saint John de Crèvecœur ("Qu'est-ce qu'un Américain?"), excerpts from the diary of Washington Irving, "Suggestions" by Edgar Allan Poe, two texts by Walt Whitman, and a selection of letters by Herndon on "the hidden Lincoln." Also included is poetry by Emily Dickinson, Vachel Lindsay, Hart Crane, Langston Hughes, Archibald MacLeish, Marianne Moore, Wallace Stevens, and William Carlos Williams. Prose pieces by Henry Miller and John Dos Passos complete the issue. The translations were done by Raymond Queneau, Fernand Auberjonois, Pierre Leyris, Philippe Dally, and Marc Le Templier, with two exception: Jeffers's poems were translated by Denise Le Fée Fardulli and Jeanne de Wronecki, and the Herndon account of Lincoln's life by Germain Landier.

The publication of *Mesures* was interrupted in the spring of 1940 after twenty-two issues. The last issue, in 1947, was an homage to Henry Church, who had just died.

In America

As mentioned above, in the 1930s and '40s trends in magazine publication in the United States ran parallel to developments in France during the same period; established periodicals generally survived the Depression, and tended to retain their initial editorial strategies. In many cases, however, there was a new emphasis on domestic (as opposed to international) issues, not only with respect to political and social matters but regarding literature as well. As a result, fewer and fewer translations were published, and translations of poetry were particularly rare. And yet in the fall of 1936, no less a magazine than the *North American Review* affirmed a new interest in poetry, as editor Joseph Auslander explained in the following statement:

It is our hope and our intention to help restore poetry to its ancient heritage and high estate. We want to help put it back where it belongs in the lives and affections and affairs of our people.

... Because the so-called "pure" poetry magazine appeals and caters to the precarious few; because, in the general magazine that enjoys a prosperous circulation, poetry is employed only as so much "filler," being abused, at best, as a sort of shabby relation, the Little Orphan Annie of the literary world; because we feel that poetry should be delivered from the Right Wing and Left Wing fanatics and given back her birthright and franchise, the natural and unfettered use of *both* her wings — the editors of the *North American Review*, commencing with the Autumn quarter, will dedicate a solid and consecutive portion of the space at their disposal to the best in poetry they can find. It will be the major motive of their policy to give substantial representation, in each quarter, to one young poet, whose talent appears to merit that distinction, as the "Discovery" of that quarter.

Auslander's wish that poetry be restored to its "rightful place" in the American literary pantheon, that it find grace in the eyes of the American public, was startling at the time, given the country's growing socio-political preoccupations. His suggestion that poets be given a more prominent role to play in American literary life was hopeful, however, and poetry did become more visible in certain literary magazines.

Interest in European literature had not entirely disappeared, and there were occasional echoes from France. For example, Countee Cullen was invited by W.E.B. Du Bois, editor of the African American magazine *The Crisis: A Record of the Darker Race*, to contribute a "Letter from Paris" to the magazine, though this did not lead to any further literary exchanges. True to expatriate tradition, some of the Americans still living in Paris (prose writers for the

The Crisis: A Record of the Darker Race (1929).

65

most part) founded journals of their own: Henry Miller and William Saroyan published *The Booster*, and Samuel Putnam, *The New Review*.

These magazines drew writers as diverse as James T. Farrell, Anaïs Nin, Michael Fraenkel (who founded the Editions Carrefour), and Walter Lowenfels, but neither of them published any French authors. In fact, they were even more isolated from French literary circles than were the expatriates of the 1920s, and the very small community had no real presence on the French scene.

Under German Occupation

In September 1939, French literary activity came to an abrupt halt. Suddenly the country was at war, and was soon cut off from the Anglophone world. French Poets and editors became soldiers, most publications were suspended, and those Americans still living in France began to think seriously about going home.

After two months of conflict, the *drôle de guerre* left soldiers with little or nothing to do, as they awaited an enemy attack. To occupy their time, they attempted to resume their usual activities, which for poets were writing and occasionally publishing. Pierre Seghers, a young poet, founded a "poet-soldier" magazine called *Poètes Casqués 39* (abbreviated to *P.C. 39*), "the first publication edited entirely by soldiers, and these soldiers were all poets."[2] Four issues were printed. The first issue was devoted to Charles Péguy, and the second to American poet Alan Seeger, who was killed at the front on July 4, 1916. He had spent two years in the French Foreign Legion, since as an American he could not join the French army, and the United States had not yet entered the war. His work was published in the States in 1917, and it was reviewed in *The Egoist* by one of his Harvard classmates, T.S. Eliot, who paid homage to the young hero and poet:

> Seeger was serious about his work and spent pains over it. The work is well done, and so much out of date as to be almost a positive quality. It is high-flown, heavily decorated and solemn, but its solemnity is thorough going, not a mere literary formality. Alan Seeger, as one who knew him can attest, lived his whole life on this plane, with impeccable poetic dignity; everything about him was in keeping.

The "poetic dignity" and the dedication to the French cause were certainly two qualities that Seghers wanted to convey in his homage issue of *P.C.*

In the spring of 1940 the *drôle de guerre* took a tragic turn, with the defeat of the French military, and the occupation of part of the country by the German army. The armistice divided the country into two zones, the northern part being occupied by German soldiers, and the southern part being the so-called

"Unoccupied Zone." Most intellectuals and artists sought refuge in the south, and those that could, settled there. Some of the latter founded new publishing ventures that would soon be at odds with the occupying forces and the Vichy government.

Demobilized, Seghers settled in the south, near Avignon, where he founded a new magazine, *Poésie 40* (which would become *Poésie 41, 42, 43*, etc., with each successive year), publishing poets from the Resistance, and participating in that movement through his journal, which became a symbol of unity and survival. *Poésie 40* was a legal publication, which simply meant that the censors could not find anything unlawful about the magazine and thus could not ban it, though they were not fooled by the editor and knew his intentions. In order to comply with regulations, Seghers could only accept French texts, and was not allowed to print any foreign literature, especially anything written in English, since one of the first things the Germans did when they took power was to publicize a list — the "Otto List" — of banned books and writers, which forbade the printing of any translation from English, except for the "classics." This policy applied to both zones as the Vichy government adopted the laws dictated by the occupying forces.

But France extended beyond its borders, and these extensions were not subject to the laws of the occupying forces. Algeria was the closest French territory, and it more or less retained its freedom throughout the war. Censorship there was less harsh, and the Otto List ignored, so those writers that could fled across the Mediterranean and joined the literary community in Algiers, where their activities and contributions helped revitalize magazines published there.

Such was the case with *Fontaine*, initially a quarterly journal that became a monthly in 1941, in order to provide a much-needed forum for poets silenced in France. *Fontaine* was founded in 1938 by the poet Max-Pol Fouchet in Algiers, and was mostly dedicated to poetry. Published in *France libre* and open to refugee writers, the magazine quickly became one of the symbols of literary freedom, untouched by the censors and unfettered by the dictates of the occupying forces. In the spring of 1940, Pierre Emmanuel, Max Jacob, Jean Follain, Jean Wahl, Saint-Pol Roux, Louis Aragon, Gertrude Stein, René Laporte, and Philippe

Poésie 41, no. 1 (1941).

Soupault were printed in *Fontaine*, which gradually became a refuge for poets of the Resistance.

With very few exceptions, the contributors to *Fontaine* were French or Francophone. On occasion, translations of Arabic poetry were included, and they constituted the major part of its "foreign" section. For the first four years of the magazine's existence, the only American text published was Gertrude Stein's "Paris-France," which appeared in the September–October 1940 issue (no. 11). But Fouchet had his eye on American poetry, and when his contributor and mentor, the philosopher Jean Wahl, sought refuge in New York, he immediately asked

him to look for contributions. Compiled before the Allied landing in North Africa on November 8, 1942, the issue was shelved until the situation stabilized the following spring. Thus, in July 1943, the readers of *Fontaine* were introduced to contemporary American writing, something not only exceptional but also totally forbidden in France. In his foreword, Max-Pol Fouchet discussed the issue in political terms, as a statement of cooperation and hope:

What was the point? To prove — and prove through action — that French thought sided with the defenders of liberty, who were defending thought itself. It was a point making our presence felt. And demonstrating, if that were necessary, that the United States, which is all too often seen as the land of Henry Ford and Hollywood, possessed a considerable literature, and that the legacy of Washington Irving, Edgar Allan Poe, Walt Whitman, Herman Melville, and so many others, was still alive. It was also a question of proving that no political climate is more suitable for intellectual life than a democracy, especially compared with totalitarian countries whose intellectuals are exiled or forced into servitude, and that only in freedom can creative minds flourish.

In his introduction to the issue, Jean Wahl insisted on the vital connection binding the two countries, the two people: "It is my wish that this issue, dedicated by France to America, by America to France, and which is published on French soil, be the symbol of an immense intercontinental continuity. To make a world today, nothing less than the world is needed." Wahl himself translated

Fontaine (1945).

most of the poems, assisted by Ivan Goll, Edouard Roditi, and Hélène Bokanowski, who contributed additional translations.

The issue included both prose and poetry. The prose section was introduced by T.S. Eliot, and featured texts by Ernest Hemingway, John Steinbeck, William Faulkner, Henry Miller, William Carlos Williams, William Saroyan, Gertrude Stein, Erskine Caldwell, and Frederic Prokosch. Prokosch was Wahl's "American connection," providing the latter with names, addresses, and translators, since he was working at the Office of War Information along with Julien Green, Edouard Roditi, Eugene Jolas, and André Breton. Prokosch also gave Wahl some editorial advice:

> *Fontaine* of course would be interested chiefly in recent work of literary excellence and of a certain experimental quality, though I agree that some established authors (Faulkner, Hemingway, Wolfe, Caldwell, O'Neill) should be included. Your list of poets also seems very sound, though two or three more recent poets might be added to show how the young writers are developing. And of course an important consideration will be the translatability of a given work — i.e. how it will look *in French* to the readers of *Fontaine*.[3]

In the end, Prokosch provided most of the texts, and rough translations that were later revised by Wahl. The range of selected poets was broad: Robert Frost, Adelaide Crapsey, Hermann Hagedorn, William Carlos Williams, Wallace Stevens, T.S. Eliot, Sara Teasdale, Robinson Jeffers, Conrad Aiken, Lola Ridge, Archibald MacLeish, Horace Gregory, Louise Bogan, Carl Sandburg, Mark Van Doren, Allen Tate, Robert Hillyer, H. Phelps Putnam, John Crowe Ransom, E.E. Cummings, Hart Crane, Langston Hughes, Frederic Prokosch, Marianne Moore, James Agee, Kenneth Patchen, James Laughlin IV, and Vachel Lindsay. The issue quickly became a symbol of resistance, and was reprinted in Paris in 1945.

To the New World

Marseilles was the gathering place for all those waiting for a visa or for transportation out of the country. It was from Marseilles that one could catch a boat to North Africa and then to America, or find a smuggler who would help them cross the Pyrenees and reach Portugal via Spain. So it was logical that when an American organization sent one of its agents to France to help European intellectuals get visas for America, they chose to send him to Marseilles. Thus Varian Fry arrived in France with a list of intellectuals, writers, and artists that he was to "rescue," attracting to the office of the Emergency Rescue Committee a community that had been scattered by *la débâcle* of spring 1940. Each Sunday André Breton, Max Ernst, Benjamin Péret, Jacques Hérold, Wilfredo Lam, André

Masson, and Marcel Duchamp would meet at the Villa Air-Bel, a house Fry rented in a Marseilles suburb, killing time and waiting for the visa that would save their lives.

One by one, they left France, Masson and Breton with his family being among the first to reach New York in the late spring of 1941. Duchamp followed a year later, one of the last French artists and writers to leave the country (though Duchamp himself was an American citizen). Just as Paris had been a hub of experimental American literature in the 1920s, so New York City became a center for French avant-garde literature in the '40s.

When poet, artist, and filmmaker Charles Henri Ford founded *View Magazine* in 1941 with the hope of promoting avant-garde writers and artists, he found it to be a relatively easy task. With the presence of so many European artists

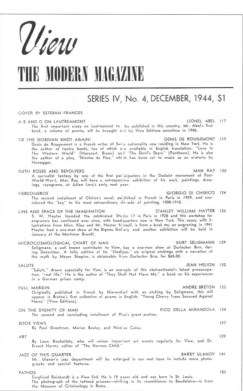

in New York, Ford was able to offer his readers an incredible publication, with covers designed by Man Ray, René Magritte, Jean Hélion, Marcel Duchamp, Leonor Fini, and Alexander Calder, and contributors ranging from André Breton to Francis Ponge, among the French writers, and William Carlos Williams, Edouard Roditi, Wallace Fowlie, Lou Harrison, Parker Tyler, and Wallace Stevens among the Americans. *View*'s initial slogan was: "View — Through the Eyes of Poets," and the magazine did focus on poetry. Though the editors did not want to limit themselves to Surrealism, and did publish many non-Surrealist writers, *View* is still considered the leading Surrealist magazine of the period, a gathering place for all Surrealists. The French played a large role, though they were published in English translation because the magazine was aimed at American readers and not at exiles themselves. Issue 7–8 of November 1941 was dedicated to Surrealism, and featured work by Artaud, Victor Brauner, Duchamp, and Masson, as well as the only interview that Breton gave during his American stay.

View Magazine, vol. IV, no. 4 (1944).

70

Ford did not create *View* in order to introduce European ideas to his compatriots, he did so to build a bridge between the two communities, and print what he thought was worth reading in both countries. Parker Tyler defined Ford's editorial policy as "making a cultural popular front between fashionable transatlantic elements and neglected aspects of American talent. ... Within *View*'s range are all the native affiliates corresponding to the imaginative sources approved by Surrealism; self-taught, fantastic and naïve poetry and art."[4]

Though *View* was a gathering place for French writers, for Breton it could never be a home. Thus when he was approached by David Hare to be on the editorial board of a new magazine with Marcel Duchamp and Max Ernst, he accepted. The magazine was dubbed *VVV*, a title that revealed the hopes of Breton: a triple victory over Nazism, social oppression, and "everything that opposed the freedom of the mind." The first issue appeared in June 1942, with a cover designed by Max Ernst. The second–third issue was published in March 1943 and the fourth one in February 1944. *VVV*, whose ultimate goal was to keep the exile community together, was dedicated to all forms of intellectual life: poetry, art, anthropology, sociology, and psychology, with contributions appearing in both French and in English. The first issue included Breton himself, Robert Motherwell, and the critic Harold Rosenberg. The second issue featured a cover by Duchamp, and Matta designed the fourth and last issue. Benjamin Péret, Claude Lévi-Strauss, Pierre Mabille, Aimé Césaire, Roger Caillois, Philippe Lamantia, Charles Henri Ford, and William Carlos Williams were invited to contribute to *VVV*, which became a reference for Surrealist writing during the war, in spite of its relatively short life span.

Just as Breton wanted his own journal, those Surrealists who were not devoted followers felt the need for a magazine of their own. Yvan Goll, who arrived in New York with his wife in 1939, wished to establish another French voice in the American city, as he had done in October 1924 when he opposed Breton with the single issue of his short-lived magazine *Surréalisme*. *Hemisphères*, "A French-American Quarterly of Poetry," totaled six issues over three years, from 1943 to 1945. Rather than limit himself to Surrealists, Goll welcomed a wide array of poets and writers, publishing Alain Bosquet, Jean Malaquais, Charles Duits, Aimé Césaire, Nicolas Calas (a disciple of Breton), Charles Henri Ford, William Carlos Williams, Parker Tyler, Saint-John Perse (who was living in Washington at the time), Roger Caillois (who had sought refuge in Argentina), Pierre Mabille, and even some writers who remained in France, Eugène Guillevic, Julien Gracq, and André Frénaud, for example. Printed in both French and English, *Hemisphères* was in a way modeled on *View* and *VVV*: dedicated to literature, it also featured artists such as André Masson, Wilfredo Lam, and Yves Tanguy. Supporting the

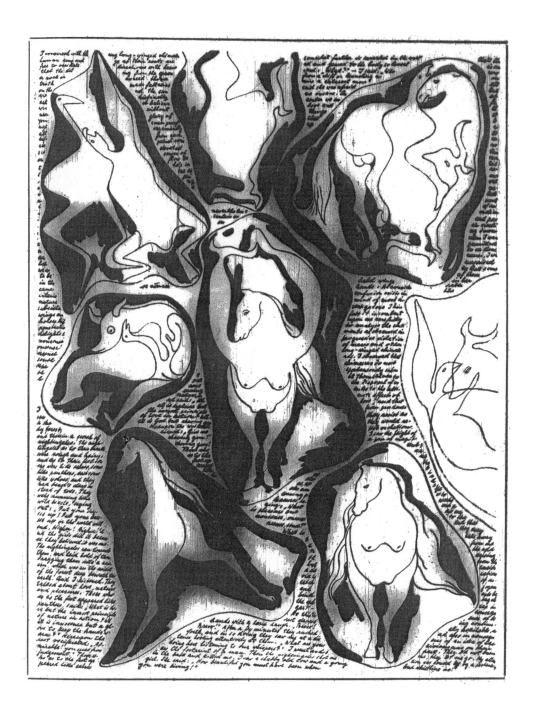

Max Ernst's "First memorable conversation with the Chimera," in *VVV*, no. 2–3 (1943).

efforts of the Editions de la Maison Française, Brentano's, and Pantheon Books, Goll and his wife, Claire, founded a publishing house bearing the same name as the magazine, printing many of the poets featured in *Hemisphères*. But both ventures ended in 1945, when most of the exiles left New York for Paris, eager to be back home and to revive the literary scene there.

After D Day

In spring 1944, the thought of D Day was on everyone's minds. No one knew exactly when it would come, but most felt that the end was near. Following the landing of Allied troops in North Africa, the French allowed themselves to believe that their nightmare would soon be ending, for in the year since that landing, the German army had lost battle after battle, and seemed on the verge of retreat. So, while some attacked the weakened occupying forces with weapons, others did so with words. One of the latter was Paul Eluard, who founded *L'Éternelle Revue* in Paris in June 1944. Considering the date, it is hardly surprising that the letter that opened the first issue was signed by American poet Stephen Vincent Benét. Benét, who had died the preceding year in New York, was a strong advocate for the entry of the United States into the war. He had lived in France in the '20s, and was both Francophone and Francophile. In an address to the French people in one of the last poems he was to write, Benét honored American soldiers who had died in France, and celebrated the friendship and solidarity binding the two nations:

> People of France, great France. … We appeal to you, for our dead are buried deep in your soil. People of France, great France we shall not betray our dead. We know how and when they died. We know that this cause is just. And we salute you, Comrade, and today our cannons speak for us. … When the tyrant's chains have been broken, his fetters split in two, you will find us at your side as friends, just as your men stood by ours, and France, great France and its children will rise up and bloom again.

Benét initiated a new dialogue between French and American poets, with Americans expressing their support for the suffering of the French people, and the

---

L'Eternelle Revue, no. 1 (1944).

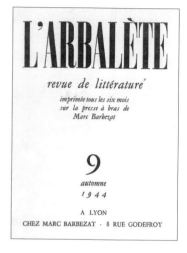

French celebrating the solidarity that prompted American soldiers to come and fight for their liberty.

Other magazines would also pay tribute to their Anglophone friends, such as two magazines published in Lyon: *Confluences* and *L'Arbalète*. In November 1944, René Tavernier, editor of *Confluences*, printed a special issue on Anglophone prose writers such as D.H. Lawrence and William Saroyan, while Marc Barbezat, editor of *L'Arbalète*, devoted its Fall 1944 issue to American prose.

Perhaps not coincidentally, there was a parallel interest in America at the time: magazines that had been indifferent to European and, particularly, to French literature during the war, were suddenly eager to assess the current situation and present what was left of the French literary scene to their readers. Thus, *Poetry* devoted an issue to French writing in October 1945, just months after the official end of World War II. "The time has come," the editors wrote, "now that France is free, to illuminate one of the particular aspects of the struggle against Germany and her minions; I mean that it is now possible to speak of the opposition of the French poets."

Founder and general editor of *Poésie 40*, Pierre Seghers was in a privileged position to contribute to this issue of *Poetry*, and wrote a piece entitled "The Conspiracy of the Poets" describing life during the Occupation. Recounting his own story, that of a soldier trapped in the collapse of the French army, of a member of the Resistance publishing a censored and eventually banned magazine, of a poet trying to hearten and motivate his compatriots through his poems, Seghers told the story of many poets who refused to give up, and who did not have (or did not want) the opportunity to leave the country during these difficult times. His colleagues and friends included members of the "liveliest and freest part of letters": Paul Eluard, Louis Aragon, Robert Desnos, Pierre Emmanuel, André Frénaud, Jean Tardieu, Max Jacob, Francis Ponge, and Michel Leiris.

These poets were for the most part unknown to the American public, and Jean Catel, still faithful to *Poetry*, briefly presented those he felt were important, in an essay entitled "The Poets Paris Is Reading." The latter included Pierre

top: *Confluences*, no. 36 (1944).
bottom: *L'Arbalète*, no. 9 (1944).

Emmanuel, Patrice de La Tour du Pin, Jean Rousselot, and Paul Eluard, and though he thought that "it was not an easy task to read them all, to comprehend their aspirations, and above all to trace the way the French muse is traveling," he celebrated the birth of a new poetry, where "a sense of fraternity is overcoming divisions," and where "Ivory towers have crumbled, and with them pre-war limitations and exclusions."

John Brown reviewed the recent anthology *Panorama de la Jeune Poésie Française*, which in his opinion was the best introduction to this "poetic renaissance." Introduced and edited by the young René Berthelé, and printed by the recently founded Editions Robert Laffont in Marseilles in 1942, this *Panorama* ambitiously presented "new" poets who emerged before 1940, and who developed as Brown's 1954 *Panorama de la Littérature Contemporaine aux États-Unis*, a seminal French-language study of American literature, which will be discussed in the next chapter.

To come to the poetry itself, the special issue of *Poetry* presented brief selections of work by three poets: Aragon, Eluard, and Michaux. Most of these pieces were translated by George Dillon, a soldier stationed in Paris at the time. While performing his military duties, Dillon "scribbled" his translations "while waiting around in jeeps and warehouses," and often without first knowing the poets themselves, simply for love of the work. In letters sent to the editor of the magazine, he introduced and defended his choices:

> These are very good in the original. Eluard's *Liberté* is probably the most famous poem of the Resistance. I thought *Zone libre* might go along with these, though it's been translated before. But *Liberté* and *Elsa au miroir* are the best. ...
>
> The Michaux poems are another group. These were also done several months ago, before I had met Michaux or knew how famous he has become here. I was attracted by what appears to be the absolute spontaneity of his poems, though as a matter of fact he broods over every word. Michaux has seen these translations and helped me revise them; he likes them and authorizes them. He is considered very important — rightly, I think, although I should not attempt to translate any but the simplest and briefest of his poems, like these. He is too subtle for any foreigner to appreciate fully, and he is just about untranslatable.

Poetry, vol. LXVII, no. 1 (1945).

In the excerpts from these letters that conclude the issue, Dillon spoke with amazement of the literary scene in Paris, and the situation of the French poet compared to his American counterpart. In one example, he gave an account of Paul Valéry's funeral, which was presented in the news as a major event, so much so that it got more coverage than the Pétain trial, which opened the very same day.

In March 1946, *View* also produced a special French issue, *View Paris*, featuring poets as diverse as Paul Eluard, René Char, Henri Michaux, and Paul Valéry, as well as a poem by Jean Genet, who also contributed an excerpt from *Notre Dame des Fleurs* in the prose section. Rather than focus on the Resistance and other war-related topics, this issue looks ahead in an attempt to determine the direction French literature might take in the postwar period. Its outlook is subsequently broad, with a variety of trends taken into account. The writers in question include — in addition to the above-named poets — Genet, Albert Camus, Jean-Paul Sartre, Maurice Blanchot, André Pieyre de Mandiargues, and Julien Gracq.

Wallace Fowlie undoubtedly had the same thing in mind when he put together the September 1952 issue of *Poetry*, which was dedicated solely to French poets. Though his selection was quite different, his goal was the same: to look to the future of French poetry as it was being written in the poetry of the day. In doing so, he insisted on the role poets had to play in redefining diplomatic relations between the Old World and the New in the postwar era: "With the possible exception of Francis Ponge, we believe that the work of these poets is largely unknown to American readers and we take great pleasure in introducing them, with the hope that this may become a practice of exchange especially in this period when a mutual understanding between countries is so much needed."

Fowlie claimed his selection to be "an innovation," because, as he said, "we are printing selections of ten French poets of today whose ages range between twenty-nine and fifty-three." Yves Bonnefoy was the youngest, Francis Ponge the oldest, and between them were Lucien Becker, Luc Estang, Maurice Fombeure, André Frénaud, Georges Guy, Jean Rousselot, and Pierre Seghers, all poets of the immediate postwar years. As Fowlie himself noted, they were reflecting on the recent tragedies and imagining the direction the world could take: "The new poetry in France seems to be following the Surrealist lesson more closely than the Symbolist, in striving, not

Poetry, vol. 80, no. 6, September (1952).

to describe any particular or personal emotion, but to reach the deepest roots of humanity. This activity often coincides with the discovery of the monstrous in man."

This issue of *Poetry* symbolically closes the period, yet at the same time suggests an opening onto new horizons. These new horizons will be discussed in the following pages, as the future of poetry in both countries moves ever closer tothe present.

Notes

1Monnier, p. 138.
2Pierre Seghers, "The Conspiracy of the Poets," *Poetry* (October 1945): 27–28.
3Unpublished letter of Frederic Prokosch to Jean Wahl, [1943]. Private collection.
4Ford, ed., p. xiii.

1950–1970 / Catching Up with Now

*I have always thought that writers everywhere should be
aware of and stimulated by each other...*[1]
— CID CORMAN

THE 1950S AND '60S WOULD SEE a gradual increase in the frequency of published translations of French and American poetry. While the poetry in question was for the most part contemporary, there was a tendency, especially in the United States, to contextualize the writing of the present by couching it in the past, suggesting that the work of late 19th- and early 20th-century French poets had not yet been absorbed in the U.S. Thus *Tri-Quarterly*'s special section on "New French Writing" (no. 4, 1965) includes work by Roland Barthes, Michel Butor, and E.M. Cioran, as well as pieces by Léon-Paul Fargue and Guillaume Apollinaire, and features essays on both the *nouveau roman* and the *calligramme*. French editors, on the other hand, stuck more resolutely to the writing of the time — whether they liked it or not (and occasionally they did not) — presenting to their readers the first French translations of Beat poets such as Allen Ginsberg and Gregory Corso, and "deep image" poets like Robert Bly and James Wright.

The emphasis was not on poetry alone, however, as prose works were also published with some frequency in magazines in both countries. Perhaps the most striking example is the American *Evergreen Review*, which published a tremendous amount of French fiction during its sixteen-year existence, presenting writers as diverse as Jean-Paul Sartre, Henri Michaux, Albert Camus, Eugène Ionesco, Alain Robbe-Grillet, Antonin Artaud, André-Pierre de Mandiargues, Cioran, René Daumal, Marcel Schwob, Jacques Prévert, Raymond Queneau, Alfred Jarry, Ahmed Yacoubi, Pierre Klossowski, Jean Genet, Georges Bataille, and Boris Vian, among others.

The 1950s and '60s also saw the founding of a number of magazines that would become known for their commitment to publishing poetry in translation: in France, *Action Poétique* (which will be discussed at length in the next chapter), and *Origin*, *Caterpillar*, and *The Fifties* in the United States.

Origin was founded in 1951 by Cid Corman, in order to give "adequate outlet to those new/unknown writers who have shown maturity/insight into their medium" and "to demonstrate the going concerns, [and] directions of contemporary creativity."[2] In this case, "new/unknown" meant not only "young/emerging," to use two current epithets; it also meant "new/unknown" *to American readers*, and in this sense emphasizes translation as one of *Origin*'s defining features.

Corman was not new to championing foreign-language poetry. He had previously done so in *This Is Poetry*, the weekly radio program consisting of fifteen-minute poetry readings, which he hosted for more than three years. Archibald MacLeish, Stephen Spender, John Ciardi, and Theodore Roethke were among the many writers to be featured on the show. A number of the programs focused on foreign-language poetry by poets such as Paul Eluard, Federico García Lorca, Gottfried Benn, and Giuseppe Ungaretti. Their work was presented bi-lingually, with native speakers reading from the French, Spanish, German, and Italian originals, and Corman reading English translations. As Corman later commented:

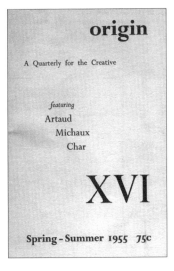

origin

A Quarterly for the Creative

featuring
Artaud
Michaux
Char

XVI

Spring - Summer 1955 75c

> I have always felt that writers everywhere should be aware of and stimulated by each other — beyond camps. And beyond special issues of little mags.... As if French poetry or that of any other country were a package and had to be treated as such — and then forgotten.[3]

Origin was certainly a testament to this belief. A long-lived magazine (it ran until 1984), it regularly featured translations from many languages, and avoided the "special issue" format that Corman found so limiting. The list of French poets published in *Origin* demonstrates Corman's emphasis on "contemporary creativity" — Antonin Artaud, René Char, Francis Ponge, Saint-John Perse, André du Bouchet, Jean Daive, Philippe Jaccottet, and Dominique Fourcade are among those he published over the life of the magazine.

Seen by some as the offspring of *Origin*, Clayton Eshleman's *Caterpillar* was also a regular forum for poetry in translation. Initially a chapbook series, *Caterpillar* began publication as a magazine in October 1967. In addition to work by Robert Duncan, Gilbert Sorrentino, Gary Snyder, and Cid Corman, among others, its first issue also included a section entitled "A Test of Translation," which would become a short-lived feature of the magazine. The "test" consisted of presenting multiple translations of a given poem, thus inviting the reader to consider translation critically by demonstrating the ways in which different translations might address the same source-language poem. About the "Test of Translation" Eshleman would later write:

> when I started the magazine ... the *quality* of translating was much on my mind, so I adapted Zukofsky's "test of poetry" and made it a "test of

Origin, no. XVI (1955).

Caterpillar, no. 1 (1967).

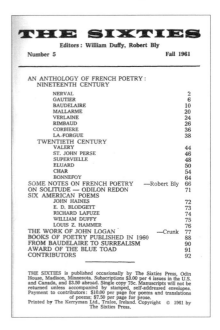

translation" and did the first two tests myself, on César Vallejo and Eugenio Montale. My idea was to set differing translations of a poem side by side and, with a minimum of comment, encourage the reader to measure them as articulations of the original poem. Behind this was a sense that we needed new translations less than we needed to know exactly what had been done in the past.[4]

The twenty issues of *Caterpillar* regularly featured translations of work by a variety of poets, including Constantine Cavafy, Rainer Maria Rilke, Paul Celan, Antonin Artaud, and Aimé Césaire, the latter two of whom would be extensively published in Eshleman's follow-up to *Caterpillar*, *Sulfur*, as will be seen in the next chapter.

Though translations were a regular feature of *Caterpillar*, the emphasis was still squarely on American poetry, "because," Eshleman reasoned, "I was convinced that it was more important for us to read ourselves in 1967 than to give the priority to translated poetry."[5] In contrast, he felt that magazines like *The Fifties* (which became *The Sixties* and *The Seventies* with each successive decade) tended "to push [translation] to the exclusion of American poetry."[6] While this is a bit of an exaggeration, it is true that *Fifties* editor Robert Bly focused heavily on translation in his magazine, which featured poets writing in Norwegian, Spanish, German, Italian, and French, in addition to English. The implication was that American poetry of the time was somehow lacking, and needed to be revitalized through contact with the poetry of other countries. As Bly and co-editor William Duffy declared in the first issue of *The Fifties*, "The editors of this magazine think that most of the poetry published in America today is too old-fashioned," and their new magazine was intended to remedy that shortcoming. In a recent interview, Bly commented on their initial editorial strategy:

> The first issue began with six poems of Gunnar Ekelöf; that was meant to prove our point. Our other strategy was simply to reject all the American poems that came in. The address being Bill's, he would gather all the poems submitted. Then once a month or so, we would drive up to Kabekona Lake where an uncle of mine had a cabin. We would open a

The Sixties, no. 5 (1961).

bottle of whiskey and send all the poems back in one night. Bill had a fantastic gift for rejection slips.[7]

In 1961 Bly and Duffy published a special issue of French poetry, entitled "Fourteen Poets of France." This micro-anthology brought together poets of the 19th and 20th centuries, most of whom reflect the editors' interest in "deep image" poetry: Nerval, Gautier, Baudelaire, Mallarmé, Verlaine, Rimbaud, Corbière, Laforgue, Valéry, Saint-John Perse, Supervielle, Paul Eluard, Char, and Bonnefoy. Their work, printed in a bi-lingual, *en face* presentation, was followed by a brief essay on French poetry by Bly himself, who also translated most of the poems. In it, he commented on what he perceived to be the fundamental differences between the poetry of the two countries: "French poetry has exactly what American poetry of the last thirty years has *not*," he wrote, "a true interest in the life below the 'world.' Rimbaud is not admirable because he took dope, as the Beats believe, nor because he shouted *Merde!* during contemporary poetry readings, though that was admirable also — but because he grasped the deep interior life flowing beneath reason."

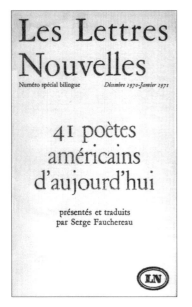

Robert Bly and four other poets associated with *The Sixties* were featured in the March/April 1968 issue of Maurice Nadeau's *Les Lettres Nouvelles*, in a special section entitled "Cinq poètes américains." The other four poets in question were Denise Levertov, Gary Snyder, Louis Simpson, and James Wright, and their work was introduced and translated by Serge Fauchereau, whose *Lecture de la Poésie Américaine,* published later that year, was perhaps the first systematic study of 20th-century American poetry to be published in French. In his introduction to the five American poets, Fauchereau succinctly describes their poetry, emphasizing its social resonance and drawing attention to its foreign influences: "These poets favor a simple, meticulous, socially motivated poetry," he writes. "They use — especially Wright and Bly — Surrealist imagery and occasionally practice automatic writing, which has come to them via Lorca, Neruda, and Vallejo. Wright has also been influenced by Trakl and Brecht."

This was not the first time American poetry was printed in the pages of the *Lettres Nouvelles*. In issue no. 4 (June 1960), the magazine had published a

Les Lettres Nouvelles (1968).

special feature on the Beats, which ran approximately 120 pages (as opposed to the fifteen pages given to Bly, Levertov, et al.). It included work by Gregory Corso, Lawrence Ferlinghetti, Allen Ginsberg, John Clellon Holmes, and Jack Kerouac, as well as writing by authors not associated with the group: Edward Albee (whose *The Zoo Story* was printed in its entirety), Charles Olson, and John Rechy. The issue also included essays by Jean-Jacques Mayoux (on the "American spectacle"), Roger Tailleur (on American cinema circa 1960), and Maria Le Hardouin (on the "discovery" of America). Given the generous selection of work presented, Nadeau's introduction comes as somewhat of a surprise, as it is highly critical of the work in question. "From a literary point of view," he writes, "they neither revolutionize technique, nor revitalize genre, and what they have to say is not particularly new." Though he recognizes the "Beat generation" as a significant social phenomenon, he is not persuaded of their literary significance, which he finds "debatable." The following lines on Kerouac sum up his views:

> The leader of the "Beat Generation" is abundant, generous, full of life, and very free. He is also occasionally verbose, confused, naïve and not as innovative as we had hoped. This exaltation of untamed America, this feeling of American space — Whitman and Thomas Wolfe have already given them to us. The nonconformity of Dreiser, Dos Passos, Steinbeck, even Sinclair Lewis was more virulent and concrete. This poetry of *vagabondage*, of sexual liberation, and these flights of mysticism — we've already seen them in Henry Miller's writing, mastered and less superficial. The language itself — blunt, full of images and peppered with slang — blossoms venomously in detective novels. Jack Kerouac apparently lacks the means of those masters he acknowledges, and if he has synthesized their influences, the mixture is anything but explosive. His great discovery of "spontaneous prose" owes a debt to the "automatic writing" of our former Surrealists, and to the confessional style and expressive techniques of Henry Miller, who is quite happy, for obvious reasons, to have found a disciple.

Only Burroughs — whose work is not included in this issue — receives what can be called faint praise ("[His] inspiration is far more audacious [than Kerouac's], and he goes much further when it comes to exploiting linguistic resources."), and Nadeau closes his essay with the statement that the Beats are more the successors than the initiators of any new forms of writing. "Their merit," he claims, "is to want to travel further along already established paths."

Some of the writers to have forged those new paths were featured in *Cahiers du Sud* no. 336 (August 1956), which included eighteen pages of "Jeune poésie américaine" by three preceding generations of poets: Wallace Stevens, Peter Viereck, Merrill Moore, Karl Shapiro, Robert Penn Warren, Richard Eberhart,

James Merrill, Archibald MacLeish, Louise Bogan, and Kenneth Fearing. This is a somewhat unusual selection, at least from a contemporary perspective, when one

considers that poets like William Carlos Williams, H.D., E.E. Cummings, and other "major" figures were not included. It is nevertheless a significant presentation of certain trends that characterized the American poetry of the time.

The poems themselves are accompanied by three essays, the first by Alain Bosquet, the second by Raymond Jean (who, with Bosquet, did the translations), and the third by René Girard. While these studies were intended to contextualize the poetry for French readers by providing socio-historical commentary, the essays by Bosquet and Jean are in fact strangely critical of the work in question, and give the impression that their authors were very much at odds with the poetry that they were presenting. For example, Bosquet's "Réflexions sur la poésie des États-Unis depuis 1945" begins:

Instability and self-confidence, incoherence and vigor, panic and vitality, excessive moralizing and impulsiveness, all of these qualities, all of these shortcomings, all of these forms of an undeniable strength and yet an obvious immaturity that we witness every day in American political activity are also present in its poetry. Not that Americans wear their poetry on their sleeve: language has never come naturally to them, and they seem to struggle with verbal expression.

And Raymond Jean's "Lieux de la poésie américaine" draws to its conclusion with the following lines:

It seems that this poetry will never ring true. Why is this? For lack of obstacles, perhaps, lack of a "hold" over the world and over men. Who can say whether contemporary American poets have not lacked — still lack — an ordeal, like the Resistance here in France, that tempers thought and language....

The consequences of this state of things brings us right back to our preamble. Incapable of a renewal of conscience, American poetry tends to seek refuge in formal solutions, in the alibi of technique. It moves imperceptibly from the creative stage to the experimental stage — not unlike a certain type of contemporary French theater: Adamov, Ionesco.

Cahiers du Sud, no. 336 (1956).

On the other hand, René Girard's "Situation du poète américain" is quite interesting for its look at the role played by the university in the American poetry of the 1950s. From the notion of creative writing as an academic discipline, to university-sponsored poetry journals, to the class of *poètes professeurs*, it traces the perimeters of an institutional poetry and for this reason remains a very timely article.

The year 1956 also saw the publication of a significant anthology of American poetry, edited by Alain Bosquet. The *Anthologie de la poésie américaine des origines à nos jours* is an ambitious work, covering American poetry from the Colonial period up through the mid-20th century. In all, seventy-two poets are presented in six sections defined according to historical periods and aesthetic tendencies. There are "The Classics" (among them Emerson, Longfellow, Melville), "The Major Figures" (Poe, Whitman, Dickinson), poets embodying the "National [or] International Spirit" (Amy Lowell, Robert Frost, Carl Sandburg, Wallace Stevens, William Carlos Williams, H.D., Conrad Aiken, Archibald MacLeish, E.E. Cummings, and many others), "Younger Poets Since Hart Crane" (Hart Crane, Ogden Nash, Langston Hughes, Theodore Roethke, Kenneth Patchen, et al.), and poets defining the "Latest Trends" (Kenneth Rexroth, Edouard Roditi, and James Laughlin, among others). The anthology concludes with a brief section on Native and African American "popular poetry."

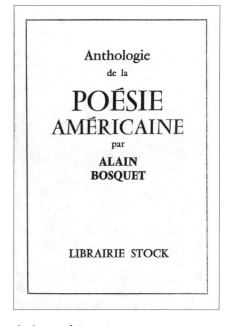

Bosquet's *Anthologie* was not the first French anthology of American poetry. In addition to the Jolas anthology of 1928, two anthologies of American poetry had been published in France in the late 1940s: Maurice Le Breton's *Anthologie de la poésie américaine contemporaine* (Paris: Denoël, 1947) and Sona Raiziss's *La Poésie américaine « moderniste », 1910–1940* (Paris: Mercure de France, 1948), the latter being a translation from the English. The publication of three major anthologies in less than ten years attests to the growing interest in France in American poetry. This was also reflected by the 1954 publication of an important study of American literature, the *Panorama de la littérature contemporaine aux États-Unis*, by John Brown. Published by Gallimard, the work focuses on American literature from the 1920s through the 1950s; in 1971 a revised edition of the book was published to include American writing up to 1970.

Alain Bosquet's *Anthologie de la Poésie Américaine* (1956).

Brown's study is an interesting one. It is organized in three broad sections, the first focusing on historical and critical issues related to contemporary American literature (with subsections on its sources, "the interwar novel," "the contemporary novel," "poetry," "theater," and "ideas"). The second section, "Illustrations," contains translations of a range of writers, from Stein, Hemingway, and Miller, to Faulkner, Nabokov, and Burroughs. The poets presented here (and we should note that Stein is listed among the *prosateurs*) include Robert Frost, Eliot, Pound, Hart Crane, E.E. Cummings, Wallace Stevens, William Carlos Williams, and Allen Ginsberg, among others. The third and final section of the book is entitled "Documents: Problems and Ideas," and includes a number of brief, critical essays by Hemingway, Eliot, Pound, Sontag, McLuhan, Cage, Mailer, and Baldwin, to name just a few. The scope of *Panorama* is, well, panoramic; it is vast, inclusive, and well done. About his *Panorama* John Brown wrote:

> There are excellent books on American literature, written by Americans from an American point of view and translated into French. There are also excellent books on American literature written by Frenchmen from a French point of view. The originality of the present book resides in the fact that it was written in French by an American with an eye to the French point of view. This is undoubtedly because the author, shuttling between Paris and New York for more than twenty years, needs both countries, whose often contradictory but always complementary qualities are so beautifully synthesized in their respective literatures.

A number of American poets and writers lived in France during the 1950s and '60s, and many of them published magazines there. As we have seen, this was not a new practice. There had been a lively community of American publishers in Paris in the 1920s, and their spirit seemed to be revived if briefly in a couple of magazines published in France in the 1950s and '60s. *The Paris Review* is the most long-lived of these journals. Founded in 1953 by Peter Matthiessen and Harold L. Humes, and edited by George Plimpton, it was published in Paris until 1974, when it relocated to New York where it continues to be published to this day. *The Paris Review* was inspired by Ford Madox Ford's 1920s *Transatlantic Review* and,

---

John Brown's *Panorama de la littérature contemporaine aux États-Unis* (1971 edition).

like it, seemed poised to become a literary bridge between the two cultures, though like many Paris-based American publications of the 1920s, it has not sought a bi-national readership but has focused instead on American writing.

Locus Solus was another French-based American magazine, and was as ephemeral as *The Paris Review* is long-lived. Founded in 1961, this handsome journal ceased publication the following year. In an unusual move, editors John Ashbery, Kenneth Koch, Harry Mathews, and James Schuyler each took turns editing issues of *Locus Solus*: Schuyler put together the first and fifth issues, Ashbery edited the double third/fourth issue, and Koch produced the second issue, a "Special Issue of Collaborations." This latter issue is an interesting look at collaborative works drawn from diverse historical periods and equally diverse cultures,

with writers ranging from Sei Shonagon to William Burroughs. From traditional collaborations such as those between Kakei and Basho, John Donne and Sir Henry Goodyere, S.T. Coleridge and Robert Southey, to more experimental Modernist collaborations by F.T. Marinetti and Francesco Cangiullo, Paul Eluard and Benjamin Péret, and André Breton and Yves Tanguy, and finally to expansive, postmodern collaborations by Frank O'Hara and the French Language; Daniel Krakauer, Aeschylus, the New York *Daily News* and a *Handbook on Birdlife*; and William Burroughs, Gregory Corso, and Arthur Rimbaud. As this list of contributors demonstrates, *Locus Solus* did publish some translations from the French which, in addition to Breton, Paul Eluard, and Péret, included work by René Char and Marcelin Pleynet.

Two years after *Locus Solus* folded, Ashbery went on to found a new magazine, *Art and Literature*, which he edited from Paris. Subtitled "An International Review," *Art and Literature* was just that; it brought together poetry, fiction, and critical writings on art as well as reproductions of artwork by authors and artists from the United States, Czechoslovakia, England, France, East and West Germany,

top: *The Paris Review*, no. 1 (1953).
bottom: *Locus Solus*, no. 2 (1961).

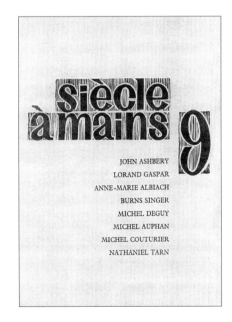

Greece, and Poland. Many French poets and writers were featured in its pages; the first issue alone contained work by Jean Genet, Marcelin Pleynet, Michel Leiris, Jean Rhys, and Georges Limbour, and its final issue presented a suite of prose poems by Francis Ponge. With its cover designed by the masterful Pierre Faucheux, and its understated, elegant layout, *Art and Literature* evokes both the editorial and graphic sobriety of *Locus Solus*. Its twelve issues were published between 1964 and 1967.

A product of the same period, *Siècle à Mains* was a French expatriate magazine founded in 1963 by Anne-Marie Albiach and Claude Royet-Journoud. Its first eleven issues were published in London, the twelfth and final issue in France. Editors Albiach and Royet-Journoud presented relatively few translations of American poetry, but what they did publish was significant. Michel Couturier's translation of Ashbery's "fragment," in *Siècle à Mains* 9 from 1967, was the first work by the American poet to be published in French translation. *Siècle à Mains* 12 from 1970 included the first part of Zukofsky's "A"-9, a poem remarkable for its formal complexity, in an equally remarkable translation by Albiach. This, too, was a first, as the poetry of Zukofsky — of the Objectivists *tout court* — was virtually unknown in France at the time, having been "rediscovered" in the United States some ten years earlier.

The publication of Zukofsky in *Siècle à Mains* in 1970 signals a change of direction in Franco-American poetic relations. It seems to herald the view that would become prevalent in France in the following decades, namely that the "experimental" tradition of American poetry was the central American poetic tradition of the 20th century, a view suggested in the United States ten years earlier with the 1960 publication of Donald Allen's *New American Poetry*. This new perspective can be seen in the reassessment and continued exploration

top: *Art and Literature*, no. 1 (1964).
bottom: *Siècle à Mains*, no. 9 (1967).

of early 20th-century American poetry on the part of French poets and translators, specifically, in the revival of interest in and successive translations of Pound's *Cantos* in the 1970s and '80s, a complete translation being published in 1986 (and republished in an augmented edition in early 2002); in the ongoing fascination with Zukofsky and other Objectivists, who continue to be featured in special issues of French literary magazines; and, perhaps most interestingly, in the apparent change of perception of Gertrude Stein as a writer, away from the author of the anecdotal works of (non-)fiction for which she had become famous, to that of challenging works of poetry such as *Stanzas in Meditation*.

The American perception of French poetry will also undergo a change of direction, but that change will occur somewhat later (roughly, in the mid-1980s), and will be more temporal than aesthetic in nature. By that time, editors, translators, and readers will have moved away from French Modernist writers — especially the Surrealists — to focus on more contemporary poets, in many cases the spiritual heirs of an earlier avant-garde tradition. Paradoxically, by this time French poetry is already reacting to its contact with recent American experimental writing and, as we shall see in the next chapter, when the two coincide in the mid- to late-1980s, it is not as two distinct poetries, each following the trajectory of its own particular evolution, but rather as two parts of what has virtually become the same poem, written simultaneously in two different languages.

Notes

1Corman, 1978, p. 244.
2As quoted in Corman, 1978, p. 239.
3Corman, 1978, p. 245.
4Eshleman, p. 453.
5Ibid.
6Ibid.
7Bly, online interview.

1970–2002 / From Neo-Past to Post-Present

> *Just as I occasionally translate American poetry myself, I also occasionally read it in English. But my real pleasure is to read it in French.... For me, translation is exactly the type of representation that I need to see and understand better [in] my own language.* — EMMANUEL HOCQUARD

SINCE 1970 THERE HAS BEEN a flowering of mutual interest in French and American poetry, demonstrated by the ever-increasing numbers of translations published in the two countries. Magazines on both sides of the Atlantic regularly feature poetry in translation, which may range from a brief selection of work by a given writer, to entire anthology-like issues of up to 300 pages or more of translated poetry. A number of important anthologies have also been produced during this time, each one offering a substantial collection of recent writing from abroad. There has likewise been a rise in serial publications, whether books or chapbooks (and in one recent case a newsletter), that either include or focus exclusively on translated poetry. Finally, with the growing popularity of online publishing, web sites have been founded with the express purpose of extending the on-going poetic dialogue between the two countries.

In tandem with the increase in publishing activities, there has been a gradual shift in interest on the part of translators, editors, and readers to more and more contemporary writing. Though literary magazines from the 1950s and '60s saw then current poets vying for pages with their illustrious (and, at times, lesser known) predecessors, over the final three decades of the 20th century — especially in the '80s and '90s — contemporary poets have all but stolen the show. American readers are less and less likely to encounter new translations of French Modernists than they are to find work by writers who may still be very new names in France. The same is true, albeit to a lesser degree, for French readers, who continue to see translations of American Modernists in their favorite magazines alongside work by contemporary American poets.

The reasons for this shift are clear: once a historical groundwork has been laid, it's possible — even necessary — to move forward, taking on the poetry of the present through a knowledge of the past. The American fascination with French Modernist writers in the 1960s and '70s helped define how American writers "understood" French poetry, just as the French discovery of the Objectivists in the same period changed the French perception of American poetry. This change of perception can be seen in the editorial evolution of magazines published in both countries over the past thirty years.

The Magazines

It seems fitting to begin this chapter with a magazine that began publication in 1970: *Invisible City*. Though known principally for translations from the Italian, this tabloid-size journal was international in scope and regularly published translations from many languages, with French poetry appearing in twenty-five of its twenty-eight issues. Editors Paul Vangelisti and John McBride tended to concentrate on three main areas of French poetry: the poetry of the late 19th/early 20th century (Eluard, Laforgue, Mallarmé, Michaux, Tzara), *poésie engagée* (Aragon, Sénac, Guillevic), and Francophone writing (Adonis, Depestre, Dib), though other contemporary poets such as Edmond Jabès, Jacques Roubaud, and Julien Blaine were also featured. Selections range from a single poem, to a page or two of work, to (in one case) an entire issue (*Invisible City* 6, 1972, was devoted to Artaud). *Invisible City* brought international poetries to American readers for eleven years, ceasing publication in 1981.

The year *Invisible City* folded, there appeared a new magazine that would do much to promote the trend of publishing poetry in translation in the United States. From its very first issue, *Sulfur* offered up generous selections of work by poets writing in many languages, mostly translations from French, Spanish, and German but also from Russian, Chinese, and Sanskrit. In his introduction to the final issue of *Sulfur*, which ceased publication in early 2001, editor Clayton Eshleman listed translation as the first of the magazine's five main priorities. "Literary magazines that restrict themselves to a national literature," he declared, "deprive themselves of the international network of information and cross-fertilization that is the heart of 20th century world poetry." He estimates that a full one-fourth of *Sulfur*'s 800 contributors were foreign writers and artists.

Eshleman's policy called for publishing both "Translations of contemporary foreign-language poets and

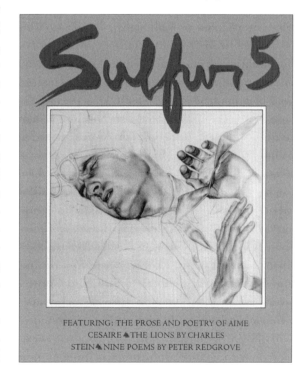

FEATURING: THE PROSE AND POETRY OF AIME CESAIRE ▲ THE LIONS BY CHARLES STEIN ▲ NINE POEMS BY PETER REDGROVE

Sulfur, no. 5 (1982).

91

new translations of untranslated (or poorly translated) older works." This approach is typical of many magazines — both French and American — which tend to feature poetry from both ends of the century, thus emphasizing a tradition of innovative writing. Accordingly, the French poets to have appeared in the pages of *Sulfur* included a numbers of Modernist writers, many of whom were either members of or associated with the Surrealist movement: Apollinaire, Artaud, Bataille, Blanchot, Breton, Cendrars, Char, Michaux, Leiris, and Péret. The contemporary poets that appear alongside them include Auxeméry, Bulteau, Deguy, Di Manno, Du Bouchet, Fourcade, Hocquard, Heidsieck, Jabès, Novarina, and Roubaud. As he had previously done in *Caterpillar*, Eshleman often published lengthy sections of a given writer's works in *Sulfur*, a policy which was also extended to translations. For example, issue 28 includes more than fifteen pages of work by Cendrars, issue 5 some twenty-five pages of Césaire, and issue 9 some twenty-seven pages of Artaud.

Jacques Darras's *in'hui* has also been generous with respect to the space it has given to translations. As Darras himself is a specialist in and translator of American poetry, it comes as no surprise that American poets have been featured prominently in its pages. Like Eshleman, Darras divides his attention between Modernist and contemporary poets, though in his case the emphasis is decidedly on the latter. Richard Foreman, Clayton Eshleman, Jerome Rothenberg, Ted Berrigan, Kenneth Irby, Paul Blackburn, Robert Kelly, Charles Olson, and Jack Spicer have all been published in *in'hui*, alongside Pound, Stein, and Williams. Presenting poets from the early 20th century in a contemporary context is both informative and revealing: on the one hand it throws light on a poet whose work may not be so well known in the target country, yet also serves to emphasize the resonance of that work in the writing of the present day.

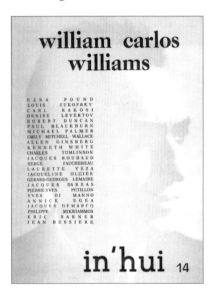

The "Williams issue" of *in'hui* (no. 14, 1981) is enlightening in this respect. Creatively edited, it includes a broad selection of writing by and about the American poet. The issue is organized into general thematic sections (*Pourquoi Williams?*, *William Carlos Williams et Ezra Pound*, *La poétique de Williams*, *L'Amérique de Williams*, etc.) and features — in addition to Williams's own poetry, which is presented in both English and French translation — essays by Darras,

---

in'hui, no. 14 (1981).

Yves di Manno, Emily Mitchell Wallace, Jacques Roubaud, Allen Ginsberg, Kenneth White, and Serge Fauchereau, among others. There is also an essay in verse by Denise Levertov, and two brief poems in Williams's memory by Carl Rakosi and Charles Tomlinson. In the final pages, Darras interviews Robert Duncan and Michael Palmer about Williams, thus closing the issue on a note that speaks to both Williams's work and its ongoing influence. This special issue is truly special; far from a basic presentation of/commentary on Williams, it is a thoughtful and insightful look at the man and the legacy of his work.

Violence II

Souléiménov Livre de glaise
Ensemble afro-américain
Hughes, Wright, Brooks, Leroi Jones, Knight
Black Panthers Manifesto
Don L. Lee Poétique noire
Jean-Claude Montel
Porta   Guglielmi
Abbie Hoffman   Eva Merriam
Jean Pierre Faye «Gewalt»
Documents de la Commune de Paris **9**

Change
Seuil

With a few notable exceptions (Eshleman being one of them), French editors seem more likely than their American counterparts to publish entire issues or sections of issues focusing on the work of a particular poet or group of poets, and over the past thirty years there have been a number of noteworthy "specials." To point out just a few:

Change 9 (1971): "Violence II," an *Ensemble afro-américain* that, in addition to poetry, includes sections on the Death of Malcolm X; the Black Panther Party; Black Poetics; and Politics, Poetry, and Free Jazz.

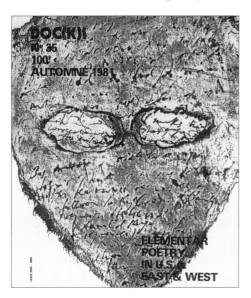

Doc(k)s 35 (1981): "Elementar Poetry in USA East & West," presenting an enormous selection of experimental poetry from the United States, including writers as diverse as Bruce Andrews, Charles Bernstein, William Burroughs, Jim Carroll, Robert Creeley, Ray DiPalma, Jackson Mac Low, Jerome Rothenberg, Paul Vangelisti, Diane Ward, Hannah Weiner, and many, many others.

Poésie 91 40 (1991): "Walt Whitman le passeur," with an interview between Kenneth White and Jacques Darras on the American poet,

top: *Change*, no. 9 (1971).
bottom: *Doc(k)s*, no. 35 (1981).

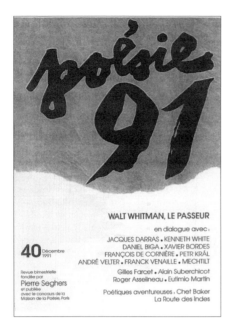

and essays on various aspects of his work, all of which are followed by a brief section on ... Chet Baker!

L'Œil de bœuf 22 (2001): "John Ashbery," a special double issue featuring an interview with Ashbery, and texts by Harry Mathews, Frank O'Hara, Mark Ford, Pierre Alféri, Pascalle Monnier, and others, with many photographs and color reproductions.

The irrepressible *Java* has spotlighted American poetry in a number of special issues and sections. Editors Jean-Michel Espitallier, Vannini Maestri, and Jacques Sivan strive to "present, gather, bring together everything that today constitutes modernity in poetry,"[1] and their editorial choices clearly reflect this desire. Issue no. 4 (1990), for example, focused on the Objectivists, and included work by Williams, Pound, Oppen, Rakosi, Reznikoff, Zukofsky, Duncan, and Corman. "Fluxus" was featured in no. 6 (1991), and was represented by Dick Higgins, La Monte Young, Ben Petterson, Larry Miller, and George Maciunas, to mention only the Americans. Issue no. 18/19 (1999) contained a special section on Jerome Rothenberg (as well as text by John Cage), and issue no. 21/22 (2001) featured a selection of "Jeune poésie américaine," including work by poets not yet published in France, among them Brian Stefans, Lisa Robertson, Lisa Jarnot, Lee Ann

top left: *Poésie 91*, no. 4 (1991).
top right: *L'Œil de bœuf*, no. 22 (2001).

Brown, Robert Fitterman, Rod Smith, and Catriona Strang.

Like *Java*, *If* regularly publishes the work of American poets, seemingly in every issue. Founded in 1992 by Liliane Giraudon, Henri Deluy, and Jean-Jacques Viton, *If* also boasts several "American specials": *If* no. 4 (1994) includes a twenty-five-page special section on Emily Dickinson; *If* no. 5 (1994) contains fourteen pages of poetry by Robert Duncan; and *If* no. 12 (1998) has a special feature on Barbara Guest, with some thirty pages of her poetry in translation. *If* has also produced two significant special issues, no. 10 (1997), the "Spécial Gertrude Stein," which contained a forty-page essay on Stein, followed by forty pages of translations; and no. 16 (2000), which was a special issue devoted to Charles Reznikoff. This collection contains translations of significant selections of Reznikoff's poetry, extracts from his correspondence, and a critical essay on Reznikoff by Charles Bernstein.

When it comes to special issues involving translation, perhaps no contemporary magazine has a richer history than does *Action Poétique*, edited by Henri Deluy. Since its inception in 1953, it has regularly featured writing by poets literally from around the world. As Pascal Boulanger has noted in his study on this long-lived magazine, "The interest in other cultures, which is manifest in translation, reveals a strong orientation that was already evident in the very first issues of *Action Poétique*.... Long before the massive influx of books in translation, the poets of *Action Poétique* were drawing sustenance from other languages, and thus straying from strictly the French literature."[2]

A brief glimpse of some eight issues published in the 1980s gives an example of the extraordinary range of poetic inquiry that characterizes *Action Poétique*:

top: *Java*, no. 21/22 (2001).
bottom: *If*, no. 10 (1997).

Issue 89–90 (1982): featuring the work of more than twenty German poets;

Issue 92 (1983): fourteen poets from Latin America;

Issue 93 (1983): fourteen Québécois poets;

Issue 101 (1984): Indian poetry;

Issue 107–108 (1987): poets from the Île de la Réunion;

Issue 111 (1988): five Danish poets;

Issue 115 (1989): Russian and Uzbek poets;

Issue 117 (1989): forty-five American poets (including Michael Palmer, Bruce Andrews, Rachel Blau Du Plessis, David Bromige, Norma Cole, Ray DiPalma, Peter Gizzi, Lyn Hejinian, et al., edited by Hocquard and Royet-Journoud).

Pierre Alféri, Charles Debierre, Henri Deluy, Emmanuel Hocquard, Raymond Jardin, Gil Jouanard, Lionel Ray, **Jean Tortel**

As the above listing suggests, American poets have benefited greatly from *Action Poétique*'s appetite for foreign-language poetry, and its generosity with respect to the time, energy, and pages it is willing to give to translations. To date, poetry from the United States has been featured in some thirty-seven issues of *Action Poétique*, nearly one quarter of the total issues published thus far (163 at this writing). It will generally appear alongside writing from France and elsewhere, but on occasion it may run as a special section, such as those recently given Mac Low (no. 144, 1996) and Lorine Niedecker (no. 163, 2001).

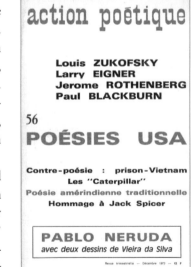

There have also been thematic issues, featuring African American poets (no. 24), American Indian poets (no. 70), and the poetry of American workers circa 1930 (no. 103). Still other issues have focused exclusively on writing from the United States: issue 117, mentioned above, entitled "États-Unis: nouveaux poètes," and some sixteen years before that, issue 56, entitled "Poésies USA."

The plural title ("Poésies USA") promises a broad palette of work, and that is indeed the case. From Modernist and then contemporary experimental poetry to ethnic and protest poetry of the period, "Poésies USA" presents a cross-section of American poetry from the perspective of the early 1970s. The issue opens with work by

top: *Action Poétique*, no. 117 (1989).
bottom: *Action Poétique* no. 56 (1973).

Zukofsky and Spicer, then goes on to present seven poets from *Caterpillar* (Paul Blackburn, Clayton Eshleman, Jackson Mac Low, Armand Schwerner, David Antin, Jack Hirschman, and Jerome Rothenberg), a selection of American Indian poetry (preceded by Rothenberg's introduction to *Shaking the Pumpkin*, which had come out the year before), and a group of poets selected and translated by Joseph Guglielmi (Paul Auster, William Bronk, Clark Coolidge, Cid Corman, Larry Eigner, Ron Padgett, and Rosmarie and Keith Waldrop), concluding with selections from an anthology of antiwar poems written by Vietnam veterans. As Jacques Roubaud writes in his preface to this eclectic collection: "This is not intended to be a representative selection ... but rather a series of texts that give brief, yet very different glimpses of significant aspects of what is currently happening in American poetry."

In that same preface, Roubaud pays homage to a man who was instrumental in bringing innovative American poetry to the French reading public of the time: Serge Fauchereau. In his *Lecture de la poésie américaine* (Paris: Editions de Minuit, 1968), Fauchereau presents an insightful study of American poetry from Imagism up through the poetry of the 1960s, with chapters devoted to Pound, Eliot, Williams, Objectivism, the Beats, Black Mountain, and the New York School, to name just a few. This seminal work offered an informed discussion of modern and contemporary American poetry illustrated with close readings of select poems presented in the original English and in French translation.

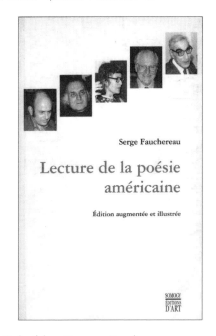

In late 1970-early '71 Fauchereau guest-edited an issue of Maurice Nadeau's *Les Lettres Nouvelles*, creating a "companion volume" to his earlier study. "41 poètes américains d'aujourd'hui" followed the same chronological presentation as *Lecture de la poésie américaine*, but focused more closely on then contemporary poets. Fauchereau's aim was to show "the different tendencies and issues that inform American poetry at a specific moment," the moment being 1970. The opening section, "Quelques aînés" (among them Zukofsky, Oppen, Patchen, and Olson), was followed by sections on the Black Mountain poets (Duncan, Levertov, Creeley, Dorn, Niedecker, et al.), "post-Beat" poets (Ginsberg, Snyder, McClure, Wieners, et al.), New York School poets (Ashbery, Schuyler, Koch), poets embodying "The New Subjectivity" (Bly, Wright, Stafford, Merwin, et al.), and

Serge Fauchereau's *Lecture de la poésie américaine* (1968).

finally, poets representing "New Tendencies" in American poetry (Merrill, Saroyan, Quasha, Padgett, Malanga, Ceravolo, Shapiro, et al.). It is all in all an impressive issue, especially when one considers that Fauchereau not only edited the bilingual volume, but also translated every poem and provided brief biographies for each poet and informative introductions to each of the sections. To quote Roubaud once again: "Serge Fauchereau's *Lecture de la poésie américaine* and his presentation of forty-one poets in the *Lettres Nouvelles* are indispensable guides for wandering through the labyrinth of American poetry, which is an immense and in many ways disconcerting territory for French readers."

At this point it seems appropriate to mention three important French anthologies of American poetry, all of which are the spiritual descendants of Fauchereau's

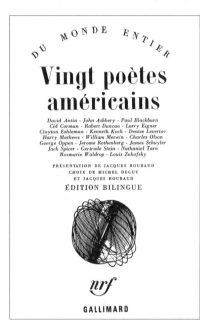

"41 poètes américains d'aujourd'hui." The first of them, *Vingt poètes américains*, was edited by Jacques Roubaud and Michel Deguy, and was published by Gallimard in 1980. It owes its editorial approach to Fauchereau (and through him, to Donald Allen, whose 1960 anthology *The New American Poetry* informs them both), for its editors present American poetry from a perspective that is both historical and aesthetic. The organization of the anthology ranges from the Objectivists (Zukofsky, Oppen), to Black Mountain (Duncan, Olson, Levertov, Eigner, Blackburn), to the New York School (Ashbery, Schuyler, Koch, Mathews). Also included are a number of poets not affiliated with any particular movement (Corman, Spicer, Merwin, Eshleman), others indicative of then recent tendencies in American poetry (Rosmarie Waldrop, David Antin, Jerome Rothenberg, Nathaniel Tarn), and one "elder" (Stein). Regarding the choice of poets included, Roubaud notes in his introduction that "our one consideration was that the poets presented here have this in common: they all play an important role in contemporary American poetry, and have not, or only rarely, been translated into French."[3]

The two other anthologies, *21+1 Poètes américains d'aujourd'hui* (Montpellier: Delta, 1986) and *49+1 Nouveaux poètes américains* (Royaumont, 1991), were both edited by Emmanuel Hocquard and Claude Royet-Journoud. Though similar in attitude and intent (not to mention in their numerical titles),

Vingt poètes américains (1980).

each one stands at a generational remove from its predecessors, the former focusing on poets who for the most part began publishing in the 1970s, the latter in the 1980s. They are also different editorially, as neither one concerns itself with the evolution of contemporary American poetry, nor do they group poets into sections based on geography or poetic schools. Rather, shared aesthetic and formal qualities determined the selection of the poets presented in *21+1 Poètes américains d'aujourd'hui*, as Hocquard would later write:

> Our only hope was to reveal ... a number of common characteristics: a priority given to language, seen as the substance or raw material for poems, and not merely as an expressive instrument or aesthetic varnish; the profusion and complexity of formal innovations ...; the mobility, freedom, and dynamic qualities of an attentive poetry, that breaks both formally and ideologically with conservative, academic models....[4]

Most of the poets included in *21+1 Poètes américains d'aujourd'hui* were unknown in France at the time. While a number of them were L=A=N=G=U=A=G=E poets, many others were not affiliated with that or any other movement. The full roster was as follows: Rae Armantrout, Paul Auster, Charles Bernstein, Mei-mei Berssenbrugge, Clark Coolidge, Michael Davidson, Michael Gizzi, Robert Grenier, Susan Howe, Ronald Johnson, Bernadette Mayer, Michael Palmer, Bob Perelman, Tom Raworth,[5] Frank Samperi, Leslie Scalapino, Ron Silliman, Gustaf Sobin, John Taggart, Keith Waldrop, Diane Ward, and John Yau.

Like *21+1 Poètes américains*, *49+1 Nouveaux poètes américains*[6] was inspired by a trip to the United States, where the editors traveled together in 1987. During their stay, they perceived that a new generation of writers had come to the fore since the publication of their preceding anthology, and they resolved to edit a new collection. On their return to France they set to work, and the initial result was issue 117 of *Action Poétique* mentioned above ("États-Unis: nouveaux poètes"), which was published in anticipation of the new anthology. As Hocquard noted, the new collection would focus on this younger generation of poets who, "without denying the experiences [of their predecessors from the 1960s and '70s], but without dwelling on them either, ... go their own way, indifferent to schools

---

Hocquard and Royet-Journoud's *21+1 Poètes américains d'aujourd'hui* (1986).

21 + 1

Poètes américains d'aujourd'hui

choisis par

Emmanuel Hocquard
et Claude Royet-Journoud

traduits par

Marc Chénetier
Philippe Jaworski
et Claude Richard

delta
1986

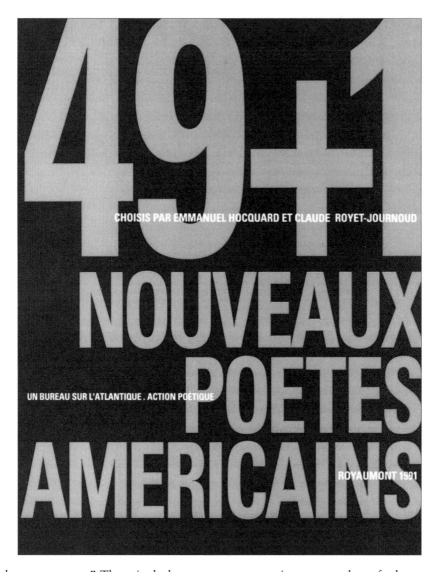

and movements...." These include many younger writers, a number of whom were from the West Coast, as well as established poets, many of them L=A=N=G=U=A=G=E poets: Bruce Andrews, David Bromige, Norma Cole, Jean Day, Ray DiPalma, Johanna Drucker, Rachel Blau DuPlessis, Peter Gizzi, Carla Harryman, Lyn Hejinian, Benjamin Hollander, Fanny Howe, Tom Mandel, Laura Moriarty, Gale Nelson, Ray Ragosta, Stephen Ratcliffe, Elizabeth Robinson, Kit Robinson, Stephen Rodefer, Eric Selland, Gail Sher, James Sherry, Aaron Shurin, Joseph Simas, Cole Swensen, Barrett Watten, Hannah Weiner, and Marjorie Welish.

Hocquard and Royet-Journoud's *49 + 1 Nouveaux poètes américains* (1991).

Though they are not anthologies strictly speaking, "anthological" is how we might describe a number of special "French Issues" of American magazines, which as a group have tended to follow their French counterparts by some ten years. While the French publications noted above date from the 1980s and '90s, several significant American special issues of contemporary French poetry have appeared in the last decade, specifically from 1991 to 2001. During this time, four very different magazines — *Tyuonyi, Raddle Moon, The Germ,* and *Poetry* — each published substantial collections (of up to more than 300 pages) of French poetry in translation.

The first to appear was *Tyuonyi*'s "Violence of the White Page: Contemporary French Poetry" (no. 9/10, 1991). Edited by Stacy Doris, Phillip Foss, and Emmanuel Hocquard, this issue brought together the work of thirty-six French poets representing roughly four generations of innovative writing, among them Anne-Marie Albiach, Pierre Alféri, Olivier Cadiot, Jean Daive, Dominique Fourcade, Jean Frémon, Liliane Giraudon, Joseph Guglielmi, Emmanuel Hocquard, Edmond Jabès, Pascalle Monnier, Anne Portugal, Jacqueline Risset, Jacques Roubaud, Claude Royet-Journoud, Esther Tellerman, Alain Veinstein, and Jean-Jacques Viton. The translations are preceded by an introduction by Stacy Doris, who charts points of intersection and divergence in the socio-cultural contexts of the two nations, tracing the ways in which these influences have shaped and informed their respective poetries. "This collection of translations offers," she writes, "an extensive group of interpretations ... concerning operative possibilities and levels of interaction between our languages."

Six years later Stacy Doris again co-edited a collection of contemporary French poetry.

top: *Tyuonyi*, no. 9/10 (1991).
bottom: *Raddle Moon*, no. 16 (1997).

"Twenty-Two New (to North America) French Poets" was the title given issue 16 of the Canadian magazine *Raddle Moon*, which Doris edited with Norma Cole. As the title suggests, the editors focused on poets whose work had not previously appeared in English translation, and, interestingly, they had the translations done by American and Canadian poets who were not translators. Included were many younger, "emerging" writers, and a few established poets, a majority of them women: Sabine Macher, Sandra Moussempès, Michelle Grangaud, Kati Molnár, Christophe Tarkos, Isabelle Garo, Véronique Pittolo, Annie Zadek, Josée Lapeyrère, Oscarine Bosquet, Christophe Marchand-Kiss, and Véronique Vassiliou, among others. As Doris noted in a postface, the selections were drawn from a "scrapbook" of French poetry she had been informally collecting over the years, "and reflect no particular generation or group of writers."

Equally eclectic in its editorial approach is the "French issue" of the bicoastal American magazine *The Germ*. Published in Summer 2001, it bears no special title, though the name of the magazine was Frenchified for the occasion (it

appears as *"Le Germe"* on the cover and half-title page). Editors Macgregor Card and Andrew Maxwell present a range of French writers, though not all of the writing in question is poetry; in addition to work by poets such as Edmond Jabès, Anne Portugal, and Claude Royet-Journoud, the editors have also included prose pieces by Jean Frémon, Michel Leiris, and Jacques Roubaud, and the issue ends with a lengthy interview of Keith Waldrop by Peter Gizzi. Perhaps the most surprising thing about the list of contributors is that so many of them are or were editors and/or publishers of poetry: there are the poet/editors of *Java*, Jean-Michel Espitallier, Jacques Sivan, and Vannina Maestri, and of *If*, Jean-Jacques Viton and Liliane Giraudon; and the poet/publishers of Un bureau sur l'Atlantique/Format Américain, Emmanuel Hocquard and Juliette Valéry. The

The Germ, no. 5 (2001).

same is true of the translators, for in addition to Card and Maxwell, editors of *The Germ*, who translated many of the writers presented here, other translators include Peter Gizzi, who formerly edited and published o-blēk editions, Keith and Rosmarie Waldrop of Burning Deck and Série d'écriture, among other things, and Guy Bennett, publisher of Seeing Eye Books.

Also included are Philippe Beck and Christophe Tarkos, who formerly collaborated on *Quaderno* (Tarkos has since founded a new magazine, *Facial*), Christian Prigent, editor of the now defunct *TXT*, and Pierre Alféri, who edited the massive but short-lived *Revue de Littérature Générale* with Olivier Cadiot, among others. Pure coincidence or conscious design, this serves to remind us that many poets are actively engaged in promoting poetry by editing and publishing it themselves.

Poetry's special double issue on "Contemporary French Poetry in Translation" was published in the fall of 2000. Edited by John Taylor and Marilyn Hacker, it features the work of thirty-nine poets, and differs chiefly from the preceding three volumes in that not all of the poets in question are French, nor are they all exponents of "experimental" writing. They include Julien Gracq, Louis-René des Forêts, Pierre Martory, Yves Bonnefoy, André du Bouchet, Philippe Jaccottet, Jacques Réda, Michel Deguy, Marie-Claire Bancquart, Jacques Roubaud, Dominique Fourcade, André Velter, and Pascalle Monnier; Francophone poetry is represented in part by Andrée Chedid, Édouard Glissant, Vénus Khoury-Ghata, Tahar Ben Jelloun, and Hédi Kaddour. The issue, which features translations by poets and scholars alike, closes with an essay by editor Taylor, entitled "From Intimism to the Poetics of 'Presence': Reading Contemporary French Poetry." Perhaps because of its breadth, both in terms of types of poetry included as well as for the many generations of poets represented, "Contemporary French Poetry in Translation" feels more like a scholarly anthology of French verse than a journal of contemporary writing, especially when compared to the preceding three publications.

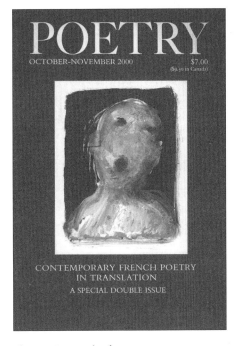

Poetry, vol. CLXXVII, no. 1 (2000).

Serial Publications

In addition to increasing numbers of literary magazines, the past thirty years have also seen an astonishing rise in serial publications in the form of both books and chapbooks. Though fundamentally different from magazines in that they generally focus on the work of a single author, they do share some important characteristics with their periodical brethren. Many chapbooks are published as a series with titles appearing at regular intervals and, like magazines, are sold via subscription. Like magazines, book series also present themselves as editorial "works in progress" in that they are frequently inscribed in a predetermined editorial context which they both reflect and amplify. At least one small press presented here — Juliette Valéry's Format Américain — promotes itself as "a sort of anthology in progress."

Of the many chapbook publishers on both sides of the Atlantic, some regularly publish poetry in translation. As with many of the magazines mentioned above, this is frequently an editorial feature that defines the collection. Such is the case with the recently founded chapbook series published by Macgregor Card and Andrew Maxwell of *The Germ*, who in their first year are publishing work by Jean Michel Espitallier and Philippe Beck along with new work by young American poets. Seeing Eye Books is another example. Founded in 1997 by Guy Bennett, it publishes four titles per year, one of which is always a work in translation. In this case the aim was to contextualize current American writing by presenting it alongside the poetry of other cultures, and in so doing to offer American readers the work of poets not readily available, if at all, in English translation. To date, Seeing Eye Books has published two North African poets writing in French: Mohammed Dib and Mostafa Nissabouri, and work by Valère Novarina and Paul Louis Rossi are slated for future publication.

The Duration Series of International Poetry, edited by Jerrold Shiroma, has taken the opposite approach. Founded in 1998, it focuses chiefly on poetry in translation, with only six of the nineteen titles published thus far

top: Mostafa Nissabouri's *Approach to the Desert Space (2001)*, published by Seeing Eye Books.
bottom: Michel Bulteau's *Crystals to Aden (2000)*, published by Duration Press.

being by American poets. The goal of this series as defined by its editor is "to broaden the conceptions of contemporary international poetry ... [and] to participate in the ongoing mapping of the international poetry landscape." French poets are prominently featured, outnumbering those writing in other languages. Anne-Marie Albiach, Michel Bulteau, Emmanuel Hocquard, Pascalle Monnier, and Claude Royet-Journoud have all been published by Duration Press. Algerian poet Habib Tengour, who writes in French, has also appeared in the series.

Though chapbooks are not as common in France as they are in the United States, there are a few small presses publishing in this format; Contrat maint is one of them. Based in Marseilles, Contrat maint was founded in Brazil in 1998 by Pascal Poyet, a poet, and Goria, an artist. They drew their inspiration from the *literatura de cordel* and *folhetos* of the South American country. Their slim volumes (one sheet of paper folded twice, plus a cover) are sold in annual series, and feature the work of writers and artists, in the original French and in translation. To date they have published work by three American poets: David Antin, Peter Gizzi, and Rosmarie Waldrop.

Of all the chapbook series published in either country, none is more explicitly concerned with the Franco-American exchange of writing and ideas than is Format Américain. Edited by Juliette Valéry, this important series focuses exclusively on American poetry in French translation, and currently includes more than thirty titles. Founded in 1993, this "anthology in progress," as Valéry describes it, offers French readers a very broad spectrum of innovative writing by several generations of American poets, from George Oppen, Jack Spicer, John Ashbery, and Michael Palmer, to Cole Swensen, Julie Kalendek, Stacy Doris, and Juliana Spahr. These chapbooks are produced in series of ten titles each, and sold through subscription. The collection is complemented by two related items: *Crossings*, a CD of recordings of some twelve American poets (some of whom have been published in the series) reading their work; and *Le « Gam »*, a micro-journal devoted to criticism and theoretical issues as related to American poetry and its translation.

Peter Gizzi's *Blue Peter*, published by Contrat maint.

Format Américain is a branch of Un bureau sur l'Atlantique, a nonprofit association founded by Emmanuel Hocquard in 1989 as part of his ongoing efforts to promote contemporary American poetry in France. His wish, as he later explained, was to "fill in the many blanks in our knowledge of that most active faction of the most recent, 'experimental' American poetry."[7] Thus it was under the name Un bureau sur l'Atlantique that Hocquard would continue to bring American poets to France for collective translation seminars at the Centre de Poésie et Traduction at the Fondation Royaumont, and readings in Paris and in

---

Bill Luoma's *Mon voyage à New York annoté,* published by Format Américain.

other French cities. It was under the name of Un bureau sur l'Atlantique that Hocquard also founded a book series dedicated to American poetry in French translation. In addition to *49 + 1 Nouveaux poètes américains,* mentioned above, Un bureau sur l'Atlantique published books by Louis Zukofsky, John Taggart, and Ted Pearson in its first four years. In 1993, when the Fondation Royaumont stopped publishing Les Cahiers de Royaumont, which presented the work of poets translated there, Un bureau sur l'Atlantique took over, and since then has published a number of other titles of American poetry in French translation, many of which were translated at Royaumont. These include books by Tom Raworth, Cole Swensen, Rachel Blau DuPlessis, Benjamin Hollander, Laura Moriarty, Norma Cole, Michael Palmer, Rosmarie and Keith Waldrop, Charles Bernstein, and Stacy Doris.

Publishing book-length works of poetry in translation in the context of a series or collection serves to define a field that effectively contextualizes the works in question for the target reader. Roughly speaking, what Un bureau sur l'Atlantique does to promote American poetry in France, Série d'écriture does to promote French poetry in the United States.

Série d'écriture is an annual series of current French writing in English translation. Founded in 1986 and initially published by Spectacular Diseases (which produced the first five titles), it has been published by Burning Deck since 1992. Edited by Rosmarie Waldrop, it includes at this writing twelve single issues, one double issue, and three chapbook "supplements." I use the word "issue" here as the publications are numbered, though Série d'écriture seems more a hybrid of a book and an anthology than a magazine strictly speaking. Nine of its titles are devoted to the work of a single author (Alain Veinstein, Emmanuel Hocquard, Joseph Guglielmi, Jean Daive, Paol Keineg, Marcel Cohen, and Jacqueline Risset), three of them present the work of many poets (among them Anne-Marie Albiach, Dominique Fourcade, Jean Frémon, Jacques Roubaud, Claude-Royet Journoud, Olivier Cadiot, Danielle Collobert, Serge Fauchereau, Liliane Giraudon, Anne Portugal, Pierre Alféri, Jean-Marie Gleize, Anne Talvez, Esther Tellerman), and the last — the double issue — is a collection of theoretical texts on writing entitled

Crosscut Universe:
Writing on Writing from France

Edited/Translated by Norma Cole

Norma Cole's *Crosscut Universe* (2000), published by Burning Deck in Série d'écriture.

Crosscut Universe: Writing on Writing from France, edited and translated by Norma Cole. The supplements feature brief works of up to 40 pages in length by Claude Royet-Journoud, Pascal Quignard, and Anne-Marie Albiach.

Both Un bureau sur l'Atlantique and Série d'écriture have much in common with three magazines that were founded in the same period: *o-blēk* and *Avec* in the United States, and *Zuk* in France. In the late 1980s and early '90s, all three journals featured work by the same groups of poets in both countries, with American and French writers regularly appearing together on both sides of the Atlantic.

Founded in 1987, *o-blēk* was a semiannual magazine edited by Peter Gizzi and Connell McGrath. Translation was a major feature of this "Journal of the Language Arts," as it was subtitled, and selections of French poetry appeared in each of its twelve issues. Emphasis was on current, "experimental" writing, as is evident in even a cursory list of contributors. French poets published in *o-blēk* include Anne-Marie Albiach, Marcel Cohen, Jean Grosjean, Emmanuel Hocquard, Edmond Jabès, Pierre Martory, Jacqueline Risset, Jacques Roubaud, and Claude Royet-Journoud. *o-blēk* ceased publication in 1993.

Similar to *o-blēk* in attitude and intent, *Avec* was likewise dedicated to the promotion of contemporary innovative writing. Founded by Cydney Chadwick in 1988, this "Journal of Writing" regularly ran selections of French poetry in translation, in keeping with its French name. Scattered throughout *Avec*'s ten issues is work by Pierre Alféri, Hélène Bessette, André du Bouchet, Olivier Cadiot, Marcel Cohen, Danielle Collobert, Michel Couturier, Edith Dahan, Jean Daive, Michel Fardoulis-Lagrange, Dominique Fourcade, Jean Frémon, Joseph Guglielmi, Emmanuel Hocquard, Roger Lewinter, Michel Leiris, and Claude Royet-Journoud, among others. Many of the latter were published together in a special, fifty-page "Section of Writing from France" that appeared in issue 3 in 1990. Chadwick began publishing books under the Avec moniker in 1992, and stopped producing the magazine in 1995.

Zuk was, in a sense, the French cousin of *o-blēk* and *Avec*, though it operated on a much smaller scale than its American relatives: *o-blēk* and *Avec* generally ran 150 to 200 pages or more, while *Zuk* consisted of a single folded sheet of paper. Founded at the same time as the former journals — its first issue is dated

o-blēk, no. 1 (1987).

October 1987 — *Zuk* appeared monthly for a period of two years. Edited by Claude Royet-Journoud, *Zuk* was a forum for contemporary innovative writing and, as its name suggests ("Zuk" for Zukofsky), it frequently presented American poetry in translation. In fact, twenty-one of its twenty-four issues contained writing by a number of American poets, many of them regular contributors to *o-blēk* and *Avec*. They include Kit Robinson, Larry Eigner, Michael Davidson, John Ashbery, Keith and Rosmarie Waldrop, Leslie Scalapino, Aaron Shurin, Susan Howe, Lyn Hejinian, Clark Coolidge, George Oppen, Louis Zukofsky, and many others.

Royet-Journoud has edited two other publications whose titles are allusions/homages to Louis Zukofsky. The first, entitled « *A* » (1978), was a magazine co-edited with Alain Veinstein; it ran for twenty-one issues before ceasing publication on the death of Zukofsky. The second, *LZ* (1981), was an anthology of mono-stichs (one-line poems) co-edited with Emmanuel Hocquard. American poets were featured in both, as they were in Royet-Journoud's many other magazine projects, which include *Llanfair* (1972–1973), *L'In-plano* (1986), and *Vendredi 13* (1992), also co-edited with Hocquard.

On the Web

Given the increasing tendency toward publishing poetry on the Internet — as evidenced by the proliferation of e-zines and poetry-related pages — it seems fitting to conclude this chapter with a brief discussion of two poetry websites: *Double Change*, an online journal focusing exclusively on French and American poetry in translation, and the Duration Press website, a resource for international poetry with an emphasis on writing from France.

Double Change is both the name of a nonprofit organization and the online journal it produces, which can be found at: <http://www.doublechange.com/>. The goal of the organization, as stated in the masthead posted on their website, is "to juxtapose, unite and reunite the poetries of France and the United States in a new bi-national, multi-faceted forum." Double Change was founded in 2000 by Omar Berrada, Vincent Broqua, Olivier Brossard, Caroline Crumpacker, Marcella

---

Zuk, no. 1 (1987).

Durand, Claire Guillot, Lisa Lubasch, Andrew Maxwell, Juliette Montoriol, Kristin Prevallet, and Jerrold Shiroma, all of whom work together to produce the journal, which features poetry, articles, interviews, and reviews, all of which are presented in the original language — whether French or English — and in translation. To date, two issues have been produced and a third is under way. Writers published thus far in *Double Change* include Nicole Brossard, Jeff Clark, Fabienne Courtade, Mohammed Dib, Damon Krukowski, Sandra Moussempès, Ron Padgett, and Christopher Edgar, to mention just a few. The online journal has a number of interesting features, for example, a section noting recent publications, a list of and links to American and French magazines and publishers of poetry, a list of reading venues in the United States and a schedule for Franco-American poetry readings in Paris (which are also organized by Double Change).

Double Change is designed by Jerrold Shiroma and hosted by his Duration Press website, which is at <http://www.durationpress.com/>. Shiroma, as mentioned above, is the publisher of a chapbook series of international poetry, but also maintains this informative website, which is a wonderful resource on poetry from around the world. In addition to information about its print and electronic publications, the Duration Press site also features an archive of out-of-print poetry books and magazines — including *Tyuonyi*'s "Violence of the White Page," discussed above — which are available as downloadable PDF files. There is also a

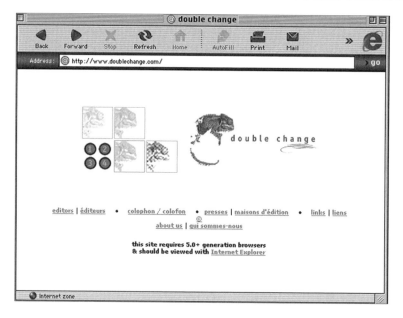

Double Change, home page.

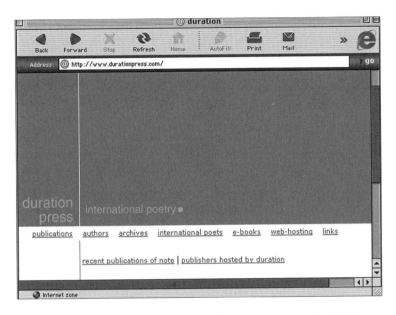

section of biographical notes on international poets, some of which feature links to poetry available electronically, and links to a number of poetry-related websites.

In Conclusion

The future looks promising for an ongoing Franco-American dialogue via poetry as published in magazines, whether print or electronic. New bi-national publishing projects continue to arise, and interest in a sustained dialogue does not seem to be waning. As this chapter was being written, two new publications created specifically to pursue the poetic relations between the two countries have come to light.

The first, « ç », is an American newsletter devoted to contemporary French poetry. It is edited by Jerrold Shiroma, and will appear twice yearly, in summer and fall (its first issue is not yet out at the time of this writing). According to its editor, « ç » will be "the only multi-author serial publication dedicated exclusively to contemporary French poetry published in America." Further information on this newsletter can be found on the Duration Press website at the address given above.

The second is the magazine *Issue*. Published in Marseilles under the joint editorship of Éric Giraud, David Lespiau, and Éric Pesty, its stated goal is to "Set out from the translation of (American) English.... Publish completed texts as well as rough drafts, writing *according to* translation." The first issue, published in December 2001, features original work in both French and English, and French

Duration Press, home page.

translations of English (USA) texts. Contributors include Jaroslaw Kozlowski, Bob Brown, David Lespiau, Clark Coolidge, Dan Farrell, Ben Marcus, and Jena Osman, and translators — who are given equal billing in the table of contents and in the running heads — include Bernard Rival, Éric Pesty, Jennifer Bonn, Nathalie Quintane, and Pascal Poyet. The issue ends with a brief note on each piece written by the translator or by one of the editors.

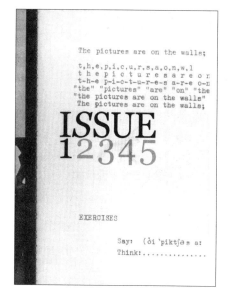

Issue suggests a possible direction for future bi-national magazines, one in which the notions of source- and target-language and -text become blurred, in which writing that predates its own translation is no longer a prerequisite. *Un travail de création* d'après *la traduction* — "writing *according to* translation," driven by the same preoccupations that drive translation, indeed, writing as a form of translation — now *there's* an idea.

Notes

[1]Grégoire, p. 90.

[2]Boulanger, p. 24.

[3]*Vingt poètes américains* (Paris: Gallimard, 1980), p. 10.

[4]*49+1 Nouveaux poètes américains* (Royaumont, 1991), pp. 12–13.

[5]From the Introduction to *49 + 1 Nouveaux poètes américains*.

[6]The "1" is for Asa Benveniste, born in the United States but having lived most of his life in England.

[7]Fondation Royaumont, p. 399.

Issue, no. 1 (2002).

Sharing Writing: Contemporary Translators Talk About Their Work

John Ashbery	Rosmarie Waldrop
Harry Mathews	Claude Royet-Journoud
Serge Fauchereau	Pierre Joris
Ron Padgett	Michel Bulteau
Jacques Darras	Norma Cole
Bill Zavatsky	Cole Swensen
Yves di Manno	Stacy Doris
Joseph Guglielmi	Juliette Valéry
Jacques Roubaud	Guy Bennett

Introduction

GIVEN THE NATURE OF THIS PROJECT, we felt it would be enlightening to invite a number of French and American translators to tell us about their work. To do so, we compiled a brief questionnaire and sent it to some twenty contemporary translators of poetry, many of whose work is discussed in the present volume. Some of them responded to our questions succinctly, others sent short, autobiographical texts. We present their unedited responses on the pages that follow.

These contributions shed some light on the whys and wherefores of translation, and also address the ill-defined relationship between translating poems and writing them. They are an indispensable complement to the preceding chapters, for without the translator, the literary exchanges that are the heart of this study would not be possible.

— GB & BM

John Ashbery

Why do you translate?

Because I can.

Whom do you translate?

French writers who interest me. Raymond Roussel, Pierre Martory, Pascalle Monnier, Franck André Jamme, Marcelin Pleynet, Denis Roche, Philippe Sollers, Max Jacob, Pierre Reverdy, André Breton, Paul Eluard, Giorgio de Chirico (his writings in French).

What draws you to their work?

Either the fact that it resembles mine or doesn't, or because I'm being paid to translate it.

How would you define the relationship between your own writing and the work you translate?

Sometimes I see curious resemblances.

Has your work as a translator influenced the way you write poetry? If so, how?

Once in a while, but in ways that I often don't notice right away and am unable to pinpoint.

What in your opinion has been your most successful translation, and why do you feel that way?

De Chirico's *Une Aventure de M. Doudréas* and Roussel's *Documents pour servir canevas*. I enjoyed translating these because both are remarkable works which are almost totally unknown. The Roussel presented difficulties since he tried to express complicated things in as few words as possible, and pushed this method to extremes. It was fun trying to approximate the original.

What has been your most interesting translation failure? Why?

I don't recall any interesting translation failures.

Do you feel that publishing translations of poetry in literary magazines is important (i.e., as opposed to publishing books of translated poems)? If so, why? If not, why not?

I don't see that it makes any difference.

What are you currently translating?

Poetry by Pierre Martory (an ongoing project) and prose by Serge Fauchereau and Pierre Reverdy. I would like to try translating Rimbaud's *Les Illuminations*.

Harry Mathews

Why do you translate?

In a very general way, I translate because I find that translation is an efficient cure for the illusion that I know anything about language and writing. It brings me back to a point from which I have to start learning everything all over again. This is particularly true of translating poetry, where the differences between languages are at their most acute, often to the point of being insurmountable.

Whom do you translate?

I translate some poets — often with no intention of publishing the results — to help me find out what they are doing and how; that is, to understand their poetry better (Catullus, Petrarch, Baudelaire, Mallarmé, Ungaretti). This motive is invariably present to a greater or lesser degree when other reasons have initiated the translations: wanting to make the work of poets I know or admire available in English, being invited to translate someone whose work I am thought to sympathize with. Friendship matters: I feel almost obliged to translate the work of someone I like as a person, provided I feel I am not rendering an actual disservice in doing so.

What draws you to their work?

I think the unfamiliarity of work is what attracts me most, its difference from what I have already read and think I understand.

How would you define the relationship between your own writing and the work you translate?

I am more interested in translation as a reader than as a writer. Sometimes I feel inspired to try out for myself whatever the translated writer is doing, but I can't remember ever actually having done that; or, at least, never directly. When Oskar Pastior got me interested in anagrammatic poetry, I used anagrams in a way he never had. All the same, I expect that in time and in some subterranean manner my translations have affected my own poetry. Very exceptionally I have taken a work translated as a direct model (e.g., Petrarch's sestina, "Qualunque animal alberga in terra ..."), but it may be worth pointing out that the model was the original work and not my translation of it.

What in your opinion has been your most successful translation, and why do you feel that way?

Of the translations I remember, those of Pastior's sestinas came out as effectively and as faithfully as I've ever managed for any group of poems. Aside from having the author's extraordinarily acute collaboration, it's hard for me to pin down a reason for this. It may be that the sestina is such a strong and supple form that it can withstand the inevitable compromises of translation with less loss than either conventional stanzaic forms or irregularly composed poetry. My best translation of a single poem was that of Pasolini's "È difficile dire con parole di figlio" ("Entreaty to My Mother"), whose success I attribute entirely to an inspiring reading of the original by Laura Betti, under whose spell my rendering forthwith emerged.

What has been your most interesting translation failure? Why?

André du Bouchet's "Sur le pas" ("On the Step"). Each word has too much resonant ambiguity to withstand the reductivity of a translator's choices: the title alone is enough to demonstrate that.

Do you feel that publishing translations of poetry in literary magazines is important (i.e., as opposed to publishing books of translated poems)? If so, why? If not, why not?

Magazine publication is *essential* as a way of giving the work of unknown writers (or new work by better-known ones) exposure in a foreign country. (This seems to work more effectively in America than in France, by the way.) Sometimes magazine publication results simply in putting unfamiliar names under a few readers' eyes: if that happens often enough, they'll start remembering the names, and if they then are interested in poetry they may take a closer look. My one regret is that poems are so rarely presented in bilingual texts. The presence of the original (even if as an adjunct in very small print) can do much to show what has changed in its transatlantic crossing.

What are you currently translating?

Rien du tout.

Serge Fauchereau

Why do you translate?

I translate purely for the fun of it, in order to share the work of writers I admire.

Whom do you translate?

I've published a lot of translations, poems for the most part, by authors writing in a variety of languages: from English into French (and vice versa, occasionally), from Russian, Romanian, German, and Spanish.

With Ron Padgett and John Ashbery New York, 1998

What draws you to their work?

I am attracted by things that are not found in French and that I want to share with readers.

How would you define the relationship between your own writing and the work you translate?

There is a complementarity between what I translate and what I write. I generally translate verse but only write in prose, though I know there are languages that do not have a prose poem tradition.

Has your work as a translator influenced the way you write poetry? If so, how?

What I translate seems to have no visible influence on what I write, but it is not as simple as all that.

What in your opinion has been your most successful translation, and why do you feel that way?

I am fond of *Quarante poèmes de Lucian Blaga* (a Romanian poet, 1895–1961), *41 poètes américains d'aujourd'hui*, and *Écrivains irlandais d'aujourd'hui*....

What has been your most interesting translation failure? Why?

I don't know. Ask my readers.

Do you feel that publishing translations of poetry in literary magazines is important (i.e., as opposed to publishing books of translated poems)? If so, why? If not, why not?

A magazine is a testing ground, a laboratory, so it is important to publish experimental and innovative writing (the very opposite of literature written for mass consumption) in magazines.

What are you currently translating?

I am translating Spanish and American poets.

Ron Padgett

Why do you translate?

I don't know for sure, but I think it has something to do with wanting to get closer to the original work, as if I were experiencing a sort of linguistic osmosis.

Whom do you translate? What draws you to their work?

I restrict myself to poets that I feel a special affinity with and who I suspect can be translated decently into American English. I've dabbled with a number of French poets, but over the years the ones I've felt most solid about working on are Guillaume Apollinaire, Blaise Cendrars, Pierre Reverdy, Max Jacob, and Valery Larbaud.

How would you define the relationship between your own writing and the work you translate?

This is a hard and large question. To answer it fully would require much pondering and gnashing of teeth. (The word "define" makes it especially hard.) But a brief answer is that I hope that some of the original poet's magic rubs off on me.

Has your work as a translator influenced the way you write poetry? If so, how?

No doubt it has, but in ways that I'm not aware of. One thing I know is that when I translate, the words, in both French and English, tend to float and fly around freely in my brain. It's a dreamy experience that I sometimes have when writing my own poems. Maybe the one process has encouraged the other. Maybe not.

What in your opinion has been your most successful translation, and why do you feel that way?

I like my translation of Apollinaire's poem "Zone" and Cendrars's poem "Panama, or the Adventures of My Seven Uncles," as well as some of his shorter travel poems. To me they sound good in English, and every time I read them I feel exhilarated and happy. I also still like the versions of Valery Larbaud's poetry that Bill Zavatsky and I did about thirty years ago.

What has been your most interesting translation failure? Why?

My failures are not interesting, to me, anyway. Frustrating, yes; for example, the way Reverdy's work seems to offer itself to English and then disappears just when you think you have it.

Do you feel that publishing translations of poetry in literary magazines is important (i.e., as opposed to publishing books of translated poems)? If so, why? If not, why not?

Books are a little better, because people tend to keep them longer and remember what's in them.

What are you currently translating?

I am slowly translating my favorite poems by Apollinaire. But since I am more of a poet who sometimes translates than a "real" translator, I take my time and work only when I have a hankering to. The selection so far is quirky and personal, with no intention of making it a selection representative of Apollinaire: *Mon Gui.*

Jacques Darras

Why do you translate?

Because I like poetry written by other people in languages other than my own.

Whom do you translate?

Poets who write in English and, to a lesser extent, in other languages (Russian, Spanish, Italian).

What draws you to their work?

Photo Jacques Sassier © Éditions Gallimard

20th-century American poetry forms an exceptional body of work reflecting on the nature of verse, and British poetry has been nourished through its contact with ancient Gaelic languages and mythologies. For these reasons Anglophone poetry covers one of the broadest spectrums of all languages.

How would you define the relationship between your own writing and the work you translate?

With my poem I stroll down Whitman's Broadway, wander over the Hexham moors with Bunting, or pause with W.C. Williams behind the wheel of a car in Rutherford, N.J. I like to adapt my gait to the poetic road traveled.

Has your work as a translator influenced the way you write poetry? If so, how?

I allow my poem to move along its own trajectory, and focus the beam of French curiosity on latitudes virtually unknown to it until now. I do breathing exercises in my language not yet adapted to new urban geologies or Jurassic strata.

What in your opinion has been your most successful translation, and why do you feel that way?

The one I enjoyed most? Whitman, without a doubt.

What has been your most interesting translation failure? Why?

More in tune physically with poetry than prose, I walk better in sustained rhythms.

Do you feel that publishing translations of poetry in literary magazines is important (i.e., as opposed to publishing books of translated poems)? If so, why? If not, why not?

I edit a magazine but oddly enough find myself preferring the book format more and more.

What are you currently translating?

Myself, into English.

Bill Zavatsky

Why do you translate?

Photo credit: © 1997 by Margaretta Mitchell

I began translating in the late '60s because nobody else was translating the poets that I wanted to read — especially the French Surrealists. My command of the French language was poor, and still is, but I persisted because, well, because it was the only way to read what I wanted to read — Desnos, Breton, Péret, Jacob, etc. ad infinitum. And I found that if translations of these and other poets *had* been made, they were generally quite awful and in some other language than American English, which is not, of course, the same language as British English. The academics, or precious few of them, who were bilingual either didn't feel a need to bring the poets that I loved into English (after all, they could already read them), or weren't poets to begin with. When *they* produced translations of poetic texts, the results were almost always disastrous.

Whom do you translate?

I have translated Arthur Rimbaud, Charles Baudelaire, Robert Desnos, André Breton, Francis Jammes, Valery Larbaud, Paul Morand (his poetry), Benjamin Péret, Guillaume Apollinaire, Blaise Cendrars, Max Jacob, Ramón Gómez de la Serna, Federico García Lorca, and have done lots of woodshed translation work. Some of these translations have been published and some haven't — and never will be. That is because some of them aren't good enough, don't please me, or have been done better by other translators. But translating what I have translated has been essential to my growth as a poet and to my development as a teacher of poetry and poetry writing.

What draws you to their work?

I began to translate the French Surrealists because my head was moving in a Surrealist direction in the '60s. They could teach me, especially, about the image, and about the act of the imagination that links anything and everything. I was then (and to an extent still am) in love with imagery and image-making. Only later, in the 20th-century Spanish poets, did I find a poetry that was deeply emotionally engaging as well as imagistically fresh and powerful. The French, for me, live too much in their heads — which is probably why they had to invent Surrealism in the first place. But the Spaniards (and Latin American poets) have more *corazón*, and that is increasingly what I think poetry needs.

How would you define the relationship between your own writing and the work you translate?

Translation and the poetry that I translated certainly fed me, opened me up, and made me think hard about how I could make Breton or Desnos *sound* like American poets. (They had to become such, you see, in American translation.) Wooden language wouldn't do, however accurate. Nor would inaccurate fumblings over meaning. Every time I hover over a page of French or Spanish (the only languages that I read with any degree of facility), I have to think, "How is this going to sound in *my* lingo? What locutions in the original have to be reinvented to work in American talk?"

Has your work as a translator influenced the way you write poetry? If so, how?

My work as a translator has absolutely influenced the way that I write poetry. The French and Spanish Surrealist poets that I have translated have empowered my imagination, meaning my ability to create images. That is why I read them in the first place, and why I continue to read them. If I am less a Surrealist now than I was in the old days (I never had a membership card!), I still feel that I can draw on the unconscious image-bank for a right picture or metaphor when I need one. Translation likewise helps the poet to get the words right, to find that one right way of saying something, and that is invaluable training for work in one's native language.

What in your opinion has been your most successful translation, and why do you feel that way?

Maybe I've caught something in Robert Desnos that I don't see in other translators' versions of his work. I'd like to think so. But a good deal of my translation work has been done in collaboration with poets Ron Padgett (Larbaud and Morand) and Zack Rogow (André Breton). In collaborative translation the first challenge (and pleasure) has been to work with another poet on a poet that we both love. So working with Ron and Zack has provided me (and I hope them) with some of the most memorable encounters that I have had with foreign poetry or, in fact, any poetry. The sense of power (there are two of us bringing everything that we know to bear on the work) and play (we really laugh our brains out in the process) has at times approached a kind of ecstacy of creation that is hard to beat. In short, I'm frequently better at being two than at being one when I translate. I like how my ego disappears when I work with another translator.

What has been your most interesting translation failure? Why?

Who wants to talk about his failures? Oh, well: probably simply not having enough time to devote to learning more thoroughly the languages that I love, and certainly not having enough time to devote to translation itself, from which one cannot make much of a living — at least not translating poetry! What these barriers mean is that one cannot attack certainly literary works that one otherwise might spend years translating. For example, I wish I had the skill and time to translate whole books of work by Malcolm de Chazal or a poet like Miguel Hernández, or to do wholesale work on Ramón Gómez de la Serna.

Do you feel that publishing translations of poetry in literary magazines is important (i.e., as opposed to publishing books of translated poems)? If so, why? If not, why not?

All of it is important. Books have the edge because they are a bit more permanent. (Try finding literary magazines on the Internet!) But in the latter case, it is terribly difficult to place books of translation with publishers; deeply frustrating, in fact.

What are you currently translating?

No big projects in the works. I teach high school full time, and have done so for many years. What little time I have for writing tends to go into my own work, though translating has always been my own work. Picking away at Gómez de la Serna's *greguerías*, mini-poems that are brilliant and hilarious. Now and again I go back to Desnos and Apollinaire, who still hasn't been done terribly well in translation except for versions by Ron Padgett and Michael O'Brien. Trying to finish an introduction to my and Padgett's translation of Paul Morand's little book of travelogue poems published in Paris in 1927 and called *U.S.A.: Album of Lyrical Photographs*.

Yves di Manno

How did I get here?

At first I translated to read better, to *hear* more clearly work I found intriguing, but that I had difficulty reading. I started translating for myself in 1967 (I was thirteen), beginning with the lyrics to the Beatles' *Sgt. Pepper's Lonely Hearts Club Band*, which were printed on the album cover.

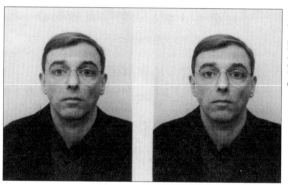

Poet & (as) Translator

A few years later, I translated the lyrics to a number of songs by Bob Dylan, undoubtedly *the* American poet (I still insist on the term) to whom I felt closest when I was young, in the early 1970s.

Somewhat later, I became interested in a more "literary" poetry, namely that of the American Modernists, who were practically unknown in France at that time (only bits and pieces had been translated). The writing of Ezra Pound was my main source of interest, as those who know my work can say. Reading the translations then available (*Cantos Pisans*, *A.B.C. de la Lecture* ...) gave me one of my first poetic shocks at the very outset of this journey: a decisive memory, to say the least, which purposefully directed my "discovery" of an infinite continent.

This and other encounters led me to translate William Carlos Williams's *Paterson* in 1979, which I did a little blindly since I had never actually studied English (or anything else for that matter), having for various reasons decided not to mix with the academic fauna. The virtually immediate publication of this translation has perhaps influenced my career, at least in part, since it made me seem the "specialist" of American poetry, which I was not. That didn't prevent me from feeling flattered when Bernard Noël invited me to collaborate on the complete translation of the *Cantos*, which was published in France in 1986.

Having completed these projects, I continued translating up to the end of the 1980s, as in my mind translation complemented the poems I was writing at the time. It was all part of an idea I was formulating then, as I wished to juxtapose other poetic models with what I rightly or wrongly perceived to be a succession of impasses, blind spots, or misunderstandings, in 20th-century French poetry.

To this end, I basically focused on the consecutive circles of those I call Pound's disciples, first the Objectivists, then the Black Mountain College nebula, and the ethnopoetics of the '60s and '70s. Interestingly, I have only rarely translated poets from the following generations, though I have read quite a few. Most likely out of lack of affinity, but also because what interested me in the American poetry of the 1920s through the 1960s was its radical difference from our own tradition. It had forged entirely new paths that had no equivalent in France, paths which I felt we might have made use of, even *a posteriori*. More than anything else, I believed I had to explore this difference for the renewal of French poetry. To be honest, the rest didn't really interest me.

That said, when practiced in such close conjunction with one's own poetic research, translation clearly has some effect on one's writing, even if this echo isn't necessarily easy to delineate. As for myself, I would say that it is in the area of prosody that American poetry on the whole has cast the brightest light on those pages I have come to write. I wouldn't call it influence — I dislike that term (I would prefer to call it an opening, a way to lose oneself in the gift of the adverse language) — but if I may make a confession here, on at least one occasion I have been decisively shattered *from the inside* by a poet from your country: when I attempted, around 1985, the French transcription of part of George Oppen's work, notably his last poems, which opened a syntactic and prosodic landscape previously unknown to me and that later enriched my own work, as it seems to me.

For many years thereafter I had to stop translating poetry, as I was drawn to an entirely different type of translation, more novelistic and thus more directly remunerative. However, two or three years ago I had the pleasure of renewing this contact by working on the *Lorca Variations* and other works by Jerome Rothenberg. And more recently, I had the opportunity to revise my already twenty-year-old translation of the *Chinese Cantos*, and create a new version of the *Drafts and Fragments* for the new augmented edition of Pound's *Cantos* that I was asked to edit and that has just been published by Flammarion.

All has not yet been said and done, but a circle has indeed just closed.

Joseph Guglielmi

It seems I've always translated. But things really picked up around 1970–1975...After a few incursions into Italian poetry: Sanguineti, Balestrini, Porta. Some friends like Jacques Roubaud, Henri Deluy, Claude Royet-Journoud had faith in me. I must say that after publishing *Aube* in 1968, I experienced a kind of crisis. And I should add that reading American poetry got me out of it: Rothenberg, Spicer, Pound, Williams, and so many others shed a new light on *reality*. And that gave *La Préparation des titres* in which I incorporated borrowings — *farcissures* as Roubaud calls them — into my writing, into the very body of the poem. So, little by little, translation became an integral part of my way of writing poetry. You can see it in my titles, *Joe's Bunker, Grungy Project, Travelogue...* Jack Spicer's *Billy the Kid* is perhaps my best translation, along with excerpts from Larry Eigner in *Travail de poésie...*

It doesn't matter to me whether translations are published in magazines or books. I don't believe in an ideal translation, but in work from one language into another.

I will add that, for me, the practice of translating is indispensable for writing poetry today...

And I will emphasize the importance of "collective translation" as it was done at the Centre de Traduction at Royaumont, near Paris. In the presence of the poet himself and a "word motor" that opens the voice. This practice, inaugurated by Bernard Noël in 1983 and pursued chiefly by Rémy Hourcade and Emmanuel Hocquard, has created a rich series of exchanges between poetries from around the world (especially American poetry) and French poetry... These exchanges are still working beautifully...

I am currently working with poet Tita Reut on a translation of *Le Livre du Témoignage* [*A Book of Witness*] by Jerome Rothenberg. A task that has given rise to a series of lively exchanges between the poet and his translators, during which the meaning was brought to light and rewritten both freely and amicably.

Jacques Roubaud

Why do you translate?

a. To understand poetry that I like.
b. To let others read this poetry.
c. To find models for my own poetry in poetry written in other languages.
Note: I also translate from French into French.

What draws you to their work?

What I don't find in my own language (cf. 1c).
How would you define the relationship between your own writing and the work you translate?

Friendly at times, hostile at others, but always difficult.

Has your work as a translator influenced the way you write poetry? If so, how?

Translating has changed the way I see poetry. Translating has directed many of my formal choices, especially the poetry of the Troubadours, ancient Japanese poetry, modern (Gertrude Stein, the Objectivists, Mina Loy, Charles Reznikoff) and contemporary American poetry, certain books of the Bible.

What in your opinion has been your most successful translation, and why do you feel that way?

None of them. My translations are only attempts to arrive at a satisfactory understanding of what I might consider to be a good translation. But I don't think I've ever managed to do so.

What has been your most interesting translation failure? Why?

All of them. See above.

Do you feel that publishing translations of poetry in literary magazines is important (i.e., as opposed to publishing books of translated poems)? If so, why? If not, why not?

Yes, of course. Often enough it's just a poem or two that you want to make available, that might not be published in book form later on. In a magazine they'll appear alongside other poems, whether translated or not, and will become living poetry.

What are you currently translating?

Some of Gertrude Stein's "Stanzas in Meditation"
Joan Retallak's "Steinzas in Mediation"

Rosmarie Waldrop

Why do you translate?

As an immigrant I am naturally *between* languages, countries. Translating is also a great alternative to fretting about writer's block.

Whom do you translate?

From German: Elke Erb, Friederike Mayröcker, Ernst Jandl, Oskar Pastior, Elfriede Czurda, Peter Waterhouse, and many others in mags; from French: Edmond Jabès, Emmanuel Hocquard, Jacques Roubaud.

What draws you to their work?

There isn't one quality (they are all very different) — except perhaps a sense of radical formal adventurousness/innovation. I have to be enthusiastic, envious.

How would you define the relationship between your own writing and the work you translate?

Mutual nourishing.

Has your work as a translator influenced the way you write poetry? If so, how?

No doubt. But I can't pin down how.

What in your opinion has been your most successful translation, and why do you feel that way?

Don't know.

What has been your most interesting translation failure? Why?

There have been many failures. They mostly uncover something so engrained in the original language that it can't travel. For instance, in Jabès's poem "Récit," the first line goes: "Il et son feminin île" — from which he is later *ex-ilé.*

The whole poem is built on this pun. "He" is incomplete without his feminine form, he is the restless sea washing around the island. "Exile" and "isle"? No, it seems forced. Whereas, for all its being invented, the formation of a feminine île from il is so within French linguistic habits that I almost wonder why it doesn't exist.

Most of the puns in Jabès's prose work have space around them for approximation and experiment, but the pun in this poem does not. Nor does it seem possible to leave the pun in French because the whole poem depends on it.

Do you feel that publishing translations of poetry in literary magazines is important (i.e., as opposed to publishing books of translated poems)? If so, why? If not, why not?

Both are important. Mags provide more immediate communication, can whet appetites. But if I get interested in a foreign author in a mag I will want to have a book, have more than a sample.

What are you currently translating?

I'm finishing up a selection of younger German-language poets for a fine new poetry magazine: *Aufgabe* (ed. Tracy Grinnell). Poets like Barbara Köhler,

Waltraud Seidlhofer, Gundy Feyrer, Ulf Stolterfoht, Elfriede Czurda, Birgit Kempker, Walter Thümler, Bruno Steiger.

Claude Royet-Journoud

Why do you translate?

To learn French.

Whom do you translate?

George Oppen (in the '60s!).

What draws you to their work?

There's something unique about George Oppen. Due to a sort of semantic instability the end of each line is both a new beginning and a break. A heightened awareness of the "little words" of the language that make up the very muscle and energy of the line.

How would you define the relationship between your own writing and the work you translate?

To translate is to write.

Has your work as a translator influenced the way you write poetry? If so, how?

?

What in your opinion has been your most successful translation, and why do you feel that way?

None of them.

What has been your most interesting translation failure? Why?

All of them.

Do you feel that publishing translations of poetry in literary magazines is important (i.e., as opposed to publishing books of translated poems)? If so, why? If not, why not?

When there's a real connection. A few examples: Stein/Roubaud, Zukofsky/Albiach, Ashbery/Couturier, R. Waldrop/Giroux, Palmer/Hocquard, etc.

What are you currently translating?

From French into French (to write is to translate).

Pierre Joris

Why do you translate?

Several reasons — that have varied over time. To begin with, I have always found that translating was the closest way of reading a poem — so as a young poet having decided to write in my fourth language (English), translating into that language was a major apprenticeship of English in relation to the languages I was translating from, and of the poets I was translating. Celan, whose work I started to translate into English in 1968, is of course the major example of this mode.

More mundane reasons include the fact that by accident of birth I was brought up in Luxembourg which meant that multi-lingualism was a fact of life — when I finished high school I had German, French, English & some Spanish (besides Latin) as well as the spoken mother tongue, Letzeburgesch. Moving between languages was thus something natural (well, natural by specific acculturation), as was the idea of translation — & then, as I came to more monolingual countries, such as France & the United States, it became obvious that translation was something I could & should do, if only simply because I had the skill (& for some time I thought I could make a living at it, which was foolish), but also, it became a sort of ethical injunction, i.e., it was something it was my duty to contribute to the community: as I was aware of, say, the superb work the Francophone Maghrebian poets were doing, it behooved me to make this work available to the somewhat language-challenged Anglophone community.

Who do you translate?

Looking back, the core of my translation work has been from German & French into English. Authors I have translated full books of include Paul Celan & Kurt Schwitters from German, Jean-Pierre Duprey, Gaston Criel, Maurice Blanchot, Edmond Jabès & Pablo Picasso from French. I have also translated large sections of work &/or chapbooks by the following: Hölderlin, Unica Zürn, & Rainer Maria Rilke (from German), Inger Christensen (from Danish), Ibn Tarafa (from Arabic), and (from French) Tristan Tzara, Michel Bulteau, Habib Tengour, Tchicaya U'Tamsi, Abdelwahab Meddeb, Abdellatif Laâbi, Mohammed Khair-Eddine, Pierre Guyotat, & Philippe Sollers. Also smaller selections — sometimes only single poems — by Stéphane Mallarmé, Antonin Artaud, René Char, Guillevic, Henri Michaux, Roger Gilbert-Lecomte, René Daumal, Jacques Roubaud, Matthieu Messagier, Adonis, Tahar Djaout, Olivier Kaeppelin, Leslie Kaplan, Yves Martin, Serge Sautreau, André Velter, Franck Venaille, and Michel Maire; Gottfried Benn, Karl Krolow, Gert Jonke, and Peter-Paul Zahl (from German); Lorca and Neruda (from Spanish); as well as texts by Giordano Bruno and Imrû'l-Qays.

During the '70s and '80s I translated a range of American and English work into French (mainly for Christian Bourgois Editeur in Paris), including books by Carl Solomon, Jack Kerouac, Gregory Corso, Julian Beck, Sam Shepard, and Pete Townsend; and, for various magazines and anthologies, smaller selections of poetry or prose by Herman Melville, Robert Kelly, Jerome Rothenberg, Kenneth Irby, Armand Schwerner, Paul Blackburn, Charles Olson, Allen Ginsberg, Thomas Meyer, Ted Berrigan, Edward Dorn, Anselm Hollo, and Robert Duncan (U.S.) and Allen Fisher, Asa Benveniste, Paul Brown, Brian Catling, Tom A. Clark, Veronica Forrest-Thomson, Bill Griffith, Ralph Hawkins, John James, Richard Miller, Eric Mottram, Wendy Mulford, Jeff Nuttall, Tom Pickard, Tom Raworth, William Sherman, Colin Simms, Iain Sinclair, Ken Smith, and Gael Turnbull (G.B.).

What draws you to their work?

A 1001 reasons — as you may judge from the catalogue of authors above. Celan most importantly because hearing his poetry when I was fourteen was what opened the possibility of poetry for me — so in that specific case I am repaying an infinite debt. But clearly most of them interest me because I think their poetry to be the best and most alive in their respective cultural traditions & languages. And beyond the individual poems themselves the poetics interest me & that means that those poets I translate are predominantly involved with exploratory, experimental poetics. I.e., I have, in a way, always translated those poets that could & in most cases eventually did wind up in *Poems for the Millennium*.

Has your work as a translator influenced the way you write poetry? If so, how?

I read to write and as translating is the closest method of reading I know of, obviously my work as a translator enters into my writing at any number of levels, from citation & collage to syntactic borrowings. I have elsewhere written about my own poetics as a nomadic poetics, i.e., a poetics that moves through languages & cultures & is not anchored in any given cultural situation or moment — & that leaves it open for translation to be an integrally informing part of its own processes. Ideally I wouldn't want to make a distinction between an "original" poem of mine & a "translation" — it's all my "writing" as all language (& thus all writing) is always already a translation.

What in your opinion has been your most successful translation, and why do you feel that way?

This is very difficult for me to say — if pushed, I would have to say my work on Paul Celan — and maybe simply because of the importance he holds for me as a poet, and the time (some thirty-five years now) & energy I have spent translating him.

What has been your most interesting translation failure? Why?

Many years ago Christian Bourgois Editeur in Paris proposed to publish a book of my work — it being understood that I would translate myself from English into French. I signed the contract, &, coincidentally, soon after moved to Algeria to teach at the University of Constantine. I figured I would have all the time needed to translate a collection of my poems over the next six months & have the book ready in late spring for fall publication. I did indeed start nearly immediately — or tried to. But I just couldn't stick to it — there was always something coming up that distracted me, something more important, a new poem to write or a party to go to, another poet to translate or a new part of the desert to explore. After four months I grew somewhat anxious about this non-doing, & tried to set up a more regular & serious work schedule, and indeed managed over a few weeks to do quick first versions of a range of poems. (That's the way I usually work — I need a first version, no matter how imperfect, but there has to be something down on paper — visible, material words in ink with which I can then start to mess. I know other translators who read & reread the text to be translated, think about it, translate it in their head & when it's ready, type out a near-final version. I've never been able to do this!) So I put all those drafts in a folder & a bit later, in another big push, started to type them up & tried to improve these initial doodles. Somewhat to my surprise — though not completely, as I was beginning to realize that there was a strange problem here — I couldn't do it. Whereas usually the pleasure of translation is in exactly that slow maturing process — the long, pleasant meanderings through dictionary after dictionary, the sounding of the translation against the original, and so on — this time it was exactly those things that drove me nuts. I had no quarrel with the badness of the first quick draft, I knew it was just a sort of vague semantic holding pattern, but grew intensely irritated when trying to find the right word in French, *le mot juste*, for what I had wanted in English. And I, the author, knew exactly what I had wanted but I, the translator, could not find the exact equivalent in French. And never did. And gave up the project & that book was never published in France. And now every time I translate someone else & claim to do it successfully, somewhere in the back of my head I have this nagging sense that I could only do it because I was not the author, because I did not write those poems in that language — the nagging sense that all translation is indeed a violence done to a text. But, I would add, a necessary violence, a violence that opens up a poem to the world, births it into our multiverse. (Poets know that and are thus usually quite indulgent with their translators — as long as it is not themselves — because they are aware that the job is impossible to start with, yet needs to be done.)

Do you feel that publishing translations of poetry in literary magazines is important (i.e., as opposed to publishing books of translated poems)? If so, why? If not, why not?

Yes, of course — in this country few books by foreign writers, not to speak of poets, are published, so magazine publication is all the more important to at least get some works by important foreign poets — the news that stays news, as Pound said — out there where those interested can pick it up. In the long run, enough people may get interested to make the publication of a whole book a viable affair. It is sad to say, but this country is growing ever more self-centered (9/11 has been profoundly misused by the powers that be to enforce this trend of jingoistic heterophobia) exactly when it becomes ever clearer that the only way out of present political & cultural dead ends is exactly by listening to the other(s). So I'll publish translations in magazines & in books, and wherever else I can — on the net and on the walls, as handouts at readings or as graffiti, whatever, as long as it gets around.

What are you currently translating?

I have just finished (in collaboration with Jerome Rothenberg) translating all of Pablo Picasso's poetic works, to be published later this year by Exact Change & am at work on another two books by Paul Celan, one of poetry, one of prose. I am also working on a range of translations of Maghrebian authors for various projects. My translation of what I consider a very important post-9/11 interview with the Tunisian poet & scholar Abdelwahab Meddeb has just come out in the magazine *October*, issue #99, as well as in the Australian online magazine *Masthead*. A book called *4 x 1*, gathering my translations of Rilke, Tzara, Duprey, & Tengour, should be out this summer from Inconundrum Press.

Michel Bulteau

Why do you translate?

To purge myself of abstract and figurative certainties.

Whom do you translate?

Writers who seem to sleepwalk on steep rooftops. Frederick Rolfe, alias Baron Corvo, Dylan Thomas, Denton Welch, and Paul Bowles, for example. Naturally, the translator might take Valery Larbaud's slogan to heart: "Dis-moi qui tu traduis et je te dirai qui tu es." ["You can tell a man by the writers he translates."]

How would you define the relationship between your own writing and the work you translate?

Incestuous.

Has your work as a translator influenced the way you write poetry? If so, how?

More accurately, my inevitable, tyrannical poetic obsessions stick monkey wrenches into the gears of translation.

What are you currently translating?

An Approach to Vedanta, an autobiographical essay by Christopher Isherwood published in 1963.

Norma Cole

Why I Translate, & etc.

It occurs to me, in the context of trying to address your questionnaire, that a question is never asked concerning the function of the translator as editor. The translator is frequently the person who selects text, translates it, and sees it through to publication and distribution. There is all the labor of translating text, but then, also the multiple editorial functions, all of which meet in a kind of detective work.

Crosscut Universe: Writing on Writing from France (Burning Deck, 2000) for which I chose texts (I'd been collecting from books, magazines, letters — bits and pieces that contribute to something like an ongoing conversation among writers over a long period of time — saving them, savoring them because I felt other writers and readers would relish the opportunity to see them) is one such project.

Other projects (*Raddle Moon* 16, for instance, which I co-edited with Stacy Doris) have involved selecting texts from a number of French writers, and pairing these texts with American writer/translators, publishing the texts as a unit indicating an array of current work from France.

The French section of *Aufgabe*, a new literary journal published by Tracy Grinnell, co-edited by Peter Neufeld, involved my editing a section of work (mainly magazines' "front matter": title pages, contents, and so on) from a range of "little magazines" published in France during the last fifty years. Although technically not "translation," this work is "exchange," an extension of my translation practice or habit.

Of course, there are times when someone simply gives the translator a pre-selected text and asks her to translate it for a specific publication or project — but so often the translator has her own ideas and rarely enough time in which to implement them all.

As for the other questions:

I translate as an extension of my own reading/writing practice; also that work be available to a readership that otherwise would not have access to it.

I have for the most part translated contemporary work written in French because I have been able to read it, and have, through making contacts of various sorts, been able to locate exciting new work.

What draws me to the texts are issues of poetics, ethics, aesthetics, their relations — in other words, all the questions of living and writing.

Of course publishing translations in literary magazines, both paper and on-line, as well as in book form, is VERY IMPORTANT so that the translations be made available to readers in all conceivable forms.

Two projects I am currently working on are (1) *The Spirit God and the Properties of Nitrogen*, a book by Lebanese poet Fouad Gabriel Naffah. Years ago, when I first met writer/painter/philosopher Etel Adnan and her partner, publisher Simone Fattal, they mentioned Naffah. On a subsequent trip to Paris I found his collected books; and (2) I am also involved, by invitation, in a project where different writers are each translating a chapter of Raymond Roussel's *Locus Solus* for the publication of the whole book by Exact Change.

Cole Swensen

Why do you translate?

To read: translation is the deepest kind of reading I know; it allows you to read a book in several directions, to get under and inside it. It makes the page a three-dimensional object.

Whom do you translate?

Several people, but they have in common that they're all focused to some degree on form, whether at the level of syntax, or genre, or somewhere in between. They're also all still living, and all relatively young; I'm interested in what French literature is doing at the moment, and how that has changed over the past several years. To follow that change is another reason I translate.

What draws you to their work?

I usually pick work that's very difficult for me — work that I have to take apart, almost down to its constituent letters, in order to grasp. This often strikes me as a not-very-bright approach, but it's the work I most want to read — work that distorts language, heightens the poetic function, and deforms/reforms genres.

How would you define the relationship between your own writing and the work you translate?

As cordial, even cheerful; at times they seem to enjoy each other's company enormously.

Has your work as a translator influenced the way you write poetry? If so, how?

I don't know — I'm sure it has, but I think the influences have been both pervasive and subtle. Except for overall structure — I know I've inherited a notion of the book as the basic poetic unit from discussions I've heard in France over the years and from the works I've translated that have been structured at the book level.

What in your opinion has been your most successful translation, and why do you feel that way?

I think the translation of Pascalle Monnier's *Bayart* — sound plays an important role in the text, and I was attracted by trying to address those rhythmic and sound relationships in English. I fell more and more in love with the text as I worked with it and learned a tremendous amount about the sound structures of French. So, regardless of its relative success as a product, the process of translating it was a constant pleasure and a constant lesson, which made it easy to go over again and again. I was sorry to finish it, and miss it like a friend.

What has been your most interesting translation failure? Why?

That would have to be *Island of the Dead* by Jean Frémon — I dearly hope that it is not a failure as a product, that it was finally "rescued," and perhaps it wasn't even, really, a failure as a process in that, again, I learned a tremendous amount — but it required a complete redoing at least twice, and largely because I kept approaching it as prose, when actually it's a very long poem. By that I mean that it didn't work to translate it at the level of the paragraph, sentence, or phrase, with an emphasis on content; it had to be translated almost word for word, or at least with acute attention to every word. And yet, of course, it is prose, with all its subtle and necessary distinctions. The whole process made me realize with horror how little I really understand prose, or even know what it is. Consequently, I had inordinate difficulty locating those necessary distinctions, honoring them, and striking a balance between the prose pacing and the poetic intensity and specificity. It was my failure, not the text's, nor, perhaps ultimately, even the translation's, and — as I said — I hope that the final product shows more what I learned and less the strain of learning it.

Do you feel that publishing translations of poetry in literary magazines is important (i.e., as opposed to publishing books of translated poems)? If so, why? If not, why not?

Yes — because it gets translation out to an entirely different and much broader audience. I'm especially glad when journals publish translations alongside American and other English-language work without marking it as "special" in any way because that works to erode the nationalistic distinctions that can arise through language difference. As is frequently suggested, American letters could use much more exposure to work done in any number of languages and from any number of countries — the political implications are enormous; they're also quite well known, so I won't go into them, but I'm always drawn to journals that go beyond strictly American work.

What are you currently translating?

I'm working collaboratively with Norma Cole on Jean Frémon's *Proustiennes* — we're working on it separately so far, and just how the collaborative process will work out is unsure, but it can't be determined in advance. The nature of the collaboration must emerge from the text itself, and I'm greatly looking forward to finding it and following it. I was interested in this project in the first place because I'd love to see the inside of Norma's process, and I know that I'll learn a tremendous amount from it. I'm also just finishing Olivier Cadiot's *Colonel des Zouaves* and will start on his new book *Retour définitif et durable de l'être aimé* in a few months, when my time opens up a bit. It's a marvelous book, and as different from his other work as each of his books is from each other. I'm endlessly engaged by his work, in part because of what he does with genre, eroding its forms toward a writing that is simply and clearly writing — a senseless thing to say, perhaps, but the work continually raises this kind of question for me; above all, I want to translate it in order to be able to read it as deeply as possible. I sometimes miss the fact that I can't do this with the many English-language texts that I would love to read as thoroughly.

Stacy Doris

How did I become a translator? In a sort of anti-social respect, the answer is that I've always been one. I remember one time complaining to some-one who wanted me to finish the translation I was doing and turn it in, that for me getting out of bed in the morning is a translation; everything is. It wearies me, and I'm a bad camper. In addition to translating for a living and translation projects to expose new French writing to American writers and vice versa; most fundamentally for me, I use translation in my "own" writing. My first book, *Kildare,* translated pop culture lexicons into a poem format. Another book, *Paramour,* uses multiple and multiplying translation techniques to level the history of prosody to an Internet reality. My most recent book, *Conference,* is a sort of version of Attar's *Conference of the Birds,* a book written in a language I don't know, Persian. I never read it all the way through, because the various translations bored me. I am now in the mortifying process of "translating," actually rewriting my book into French, in the hope that it can get translated back, with huge censorship of course (another form of translation), into Farsi some day. And I have written two books in French, *La Vie de Chester Steven Wiener écrite par sa femme,* and *Une Année à New York avec Chester.* They are not translations, but rather impact English on French. Actually, what you are reading here (mostly in the paragraph to come) is the closest of anything I've ever written in English to my writing in French. Except that I can let myself go more in French, because there is a sort of cultural attention span on the part of French readers. And there is a pertinent tension in French/France between spoken and written language which makes it fun for me to vacillate between Stendhal style and street talk. And I have the thrill of making English push through into French, like a layer of underpaint or overpaint, sandwiching the two languages; showing French some potential it might not always realize it has. But what I learned from it all is that French is my mother tongue. Because the way I write in French follows the Baroque narrative lines and tricky syntax of the kind of story my mother tells me on the phone. So which is the translation then, English or French?

Generally, I see my role as a translator as a kind of social engagement. Because of all the time I have spent hanging out in France, I have more direct access to new writing in French, and what I try to do is coordinate things so that developments in North America and in France meet through direct translating encounters between writers. I try to set it up, like a dating service. I take on some special projects for myself though. Currently, I am about to translate some work by Ryoko Sekiguchi. She writes in Japanese and has "faithfully," according to her, translated her own work into French. There is also a slight Farsi layer to it. So I like the idea of translating this into English (from French). For obvious reasons, I avoid translating or asking others to translate work by writers that have already appeared in translation. Another current project in which I am really just a go-between is a translation of part of Harryete Mullen's *Muse & Drudge*. The online magazine *Double Change* asked me if I would translate Mullen. Instead of taking on that near-impossibility, I offered to find a French poet to do it, and help out if needed. So Sébastien Smirou is translating Harryette Mullen and I am just watching. I like this kind of scale and intervention. For years, at my instigation, Anne Portugal has been translating a few pages of writing by Caroline Bergvall, and I have a promise from the French magazine *Java* to publish it, though it may never come to that. Socially speaking, my adventures as a translator, or more importantly, as I see it, as a coordinator of translations, began when Chet Wiener and I landed in Paris for our first long-term stay, in 1989. Friends in America had told us there would be some sort of Objectivist conference at some castle or other not far from Paris, starting on the day after our arrival. We'd heard that our idols, whom we'd never met, Michael Palmer, Lyn Hejinian, and Charles Bernstein, would be there. Somehow we managed to turn up at the abbaye de Royaumont, where the event was indeed under way. There, in addition to the aforementioned idols, we were smack in the company of many of the major French poets of our time, including Anne-Marie Albiach, Claude Royet-Journoud, Joseph Guglielmi, and others. A party. I had never heard of these important French poets, and my French was quite basic. I knew Spanish, and had thought I could just pick French up by starting to read books in the language, and getting grammar and pronunciation tips from would-be gigolos who hung out in the cafés of Marrakech, where I had gone for an extended stay partly with the crazy idea of improving my nonexistent French. For my reading, I started out with a few basics such as *Candide* and Wittig's *Les Guerillères*, picked up at the French Cultural Center of Marrakech, before moving on to *À la recherche du temps perdu*, which seemed like a perfect choice since I had read the thing one and a half times already in English, and knew the story. I was still working my way through Proust with a dictionary when I left Marrakech for Iowa City, where I immediately enrolled in a graduate-level French literature course. The professor was really nice and I luckily had picked a 17th-century survey the first time out. But writing the three papers in French was dumbfounding. Anyhow, back at the Cistercian abbey, Michael Palmer took it upon himself to ask around among the French greats present if they knew of any *chambres de bonne* that any young Americans on a small grant (that was me and Chet; he had a Fulbright Teaching Fellowship; and really, Fulbright should try paying enough for someone to live off) could rent for cheap. This made for an excellent overall impression in our favor. I immediately approached the great French poet I'd never heard of, Emmanuel Hocquard, and asked him if he would co-edit a French poetry issue for an American magazine run out of a teepee in New Mexico with me, and he immediately agreed. The journal was *Tyuonyi*, just about the only place that had gone so far as to publish my work up until then. And the anthology issue, *Violence of the White Page*, was thanks to all Emmanuel's work, while I sat back and finally got some clues. I remember hiding out in libraries and bookstores with piles of books, skimming and mulling and tentatively choosing. But my real job was figuring out what might have been translated, by whom, and putting American poet translators together with French poets. I felt like a party planner. Or Girl Scout troop leader. It was in this spirit, and with pressure from American poet readers ("okay, but where is the really NEW French poetry") in the light of my French poet friends' responses ("no, there is really nothing interesting happening these days"), that I began to bring writing together by about fifty emerging French poets, many of whom had never published. The resulting archive, on deposit in a few American spots, proved useful for several projects, both failed and realized, such as providing material for the issue of *Raddle Moon* I co-edited with Norma Cole, *Twenty-two New (to North America) French Poets*, and bringing me into contact with the then unpublished Christophe Tarkos, who has since (since 1995) written nearly thirty books and become a phenomenon. Chet and I recently co-edited the first collection of his work in English: *Christophe Tarkos: Ma Langue Est Poétique — Selected Work* (New York: Roof, 2001). And for an anthology of this new French writing, which was commissioned but never appeared, I wrote my first piece in French ever, in Girl Scout troop leader style. The friends I showed it to help me correct the grammar, Olivier Cadiot and Pierre Alféri, were so tickled that they commissioned me to write a longer piece along the same lines for their magazine, *Revue de Littérature Générale*. And that is how I became a French writer.

Juliette Valéry

Why do you translate? — How would you define the relationship between your own writing and the work you translate?

I translate to write. Translation is my main writing activity. I use the same approach in my visual and sound work, even in my current teaching in an art school. In fact, I consider all of these activities types of translation. I translate to read, then to copy and transmit as attentively as possible, from wherever I might be at the moment. (Actually, teaching is a bit different because I am much more aware of my immediate audience.) For me, translation is also an opportunity to engage in collective work: with the author, during collective translation seminars that we (Un bureau sur l'Atlantique) organize; if not, in correspondence with him, and always with readers — that's an important dimension.

The design of the books I publish in Format Américain is also a kind of translation: for example, for Jena Osman's chapbook, *Tableau périodique des éléments réagencé par le Dr. Jivago, oculiste*, I had to find a "physical" solution to translate into book form a work conceived in CD-ROM format, with links, poem-definitions, and images. Or for Lisa Jarnot's *Libretto Marin*, I "translated" the Golden Gate Bridge that appears on the cover of the American book — a heavily pixelated negative image — by creating a blurry print of the bridge from a picture I had taken.

Whom do you translate? What draws you to their work?

I basically translate American writers, whom I also publish. My choice of authors is difficult to explain. It is fairly subjective in that the possibilities are unlimited, and certainly beyond the scope of the project of a small structure like Un bureau sur l'Atlantique, which is in fact a type of surf board. But the "subject" is multiple. Bill Luoma introduced me to *Experiments* by Bernadette Mayer, Juliana Spahr, and Lisa Jarnot. Each translation has its rhizome story, which moves through networks that are both friendly and critical. Book exchanges, trips, friendships, love stories. Rumor also plays a part, like a way of circulating texts. The Internet is a broad vector of rumors.

I choose work to translate according to diverse criteria related to its publication: a magazine when I am asked to, a Format Américain-style chapbook, a longer book. I am also attracted by difficulty: the constraint of six words per line in Bob Perelman's *Marginalization of Poetry*, the interchangeable subject in Lisa Jarnot's work, the sound poetry of Jackson Mac Low. In fact, things that appear untranslatable I find particularly exciting.

What in your opinion has been your most successful translation, and why do you feel that way? / What has been your most interesting translation failure? Why?

I really can't answer these questions. I feel pangs of "remorse" over little details, for example when I discover a false cognate that I hadn't seen three years before.

143

But I can always correct the texts (especially in Format Américain, with each new edition).

Do you feel that publishing translations of poetry in literary magazines is important (i.e., as opposed to publishing books of translated poems)? If so, why? If not, why not?

Yes, but the same is true of books. Unfortunately, not many French publishers regularly publish translations. The role of magazines is also very important; they have the advantage of bringing authors from both countries together.

Whom are you currently translating?

Lisa Lubasch and Rod Smith.

Guy Bennett

Why do you translate?

To get closer to a poem that intrigues me, to get inside it, take it apart, see how it works and maybe figure out what exactly appeals to me.

Whom do you translate?

Preferably poets whose work in one way or another challenges traditional notions of poetry, writing, or language. Early Modernists like Marinetti and Kruchenykh; contemporaries like Giovanna Sandri and Michelle Grangaud. It seems to me that the concerns raised by the former are still resonating in the work of the latter.

What draws you to their work?

Its singularity. The fact that it would be difficult to translate. The fact that it appeals to me as poetry.

How would you define the relationship between your own writing and the work you translate?

Cannibalistic. Inevitably, the work I translate comes to nourish my own writing, whether unconsciously (because there was some similarity there to begin with and the act of translating only makes that more apparent) or consciously (i.e., that I go at it in order to make mine what I find exciting in someone else's work).

Has your work as a translator influenced the way you write poetry? If so, how?

I think that it's broadened my conception of writing, and is either the cause or reflection of my tendency to work from some sort of source text, be it poetry (as in my first book, *Last Words*), artists' writings (as in *The Row*, my second book), or scholarly texts (as in *One Hundred Famous Views*, my most recent collection).

What in your opinion has been your most successful translation, and why do you feel that way?

I'm not sure any of them have been truly successful, if what we mean by that is that I got it right and couldn't do better. Looking back over translations I've done — even the recent ones — I always find things that in retrospect don't work as well as I had thought or that could have been done differently. I accept this as part of the process. To paraphrase Valéry, "You don't finish a translation; you abandon it."

What has been your most interesting translation failure? Why?

I don't know. Some poems by Breton, maybe, translated while I was still in graduate school. I showed them to a translation teacher I had. He told me that when he'd first read them, he found them really bad. Then he went back and reread the French originals and told me that they weren't very good either, though that didn't make my translations any better. (Admittedly, he was not a lover of Surrealist verse.)

Do you feel that publishing translations of poetry in literary magazines is important (i.e., as opposed to publishing books of translated poems)? If so, why? If not, why not?

Yes, I do. It's an opportunity to "get the word out" quickly to readers who might not otherwise ever hear of the poets in question. It's also easier to publish a handful of translated poems in a magazine than it is to find a publisher to bring out the book (though the current chapbook craze may be changing that). All of which means that more poetry gets out to more people more quickly. And to paraphrase Mies van der Rohe, "More is more."

What are you currently translating?

Poésie, etcetera: *ménage*, by Jacques Roubaud
A section from *Faïences*, by Paul Louis Rossi
"Le Monologue d'Adramélech," by Valère Novarina

Some Notes on French Literature at The New York Public Library

by Rodney Phillips

Director, Humanities and Social Sciences Library,
The New York Public Library

T HE NEW YORK PUBLIC LIBRARY has over the last one hundred years actively collected books and serials published in France, and the collections related to French language and literature are among the strongest in the Library. The founding Astor Library contained slightly more than 3,000 volumes of French literature, but by 1921 the number had increased to 23,000 and in 1966 there were nearly 50,000 volumes (current estimates would double this figure).

Early Manuscripts and Printed Books

Among the earliest materials is a 10th-century Lectionary from France. Other illuminated manuscripts include a heavily illustrated volume of Bible stories and the lives of saints from 1200 and a manuscript copy of the *Petit Artus de Bretaigne*, illuminated in the mid-1400s for the duc de Nemours, one Jacques d'Armagnac. A bibliography of early French books (printed before 1651) lists more than 1,300 titles in the collections, including the first Bible printed in Paris, in 1476, and a Bible printed in Lyon in 1477 by the great Guillaume de Roy. Of the Library's nearly thirty-five incunabula published in France, some volumes of note include a Boccaccio published in Strasbourg in 1474, an *Ars Moriendi* published in Lyon in 1490, Guillaume de Deguileville's *El Pelegrino dela Vida Humana*, published in 1490 in Toulouse, and a copy of Sebastian Brant's *Stultifera Navis* (*Ship of Fools*) published in Lyon in 1498. The Library has no early printings of the works of Villon, but more than a hundred later editions and translations.

The 16th Century, the Renaissance, and the Pléiade

The great French printers of the 16th century (the Estiennes, Simon de Colines, and Michel Vascosan) are very well represented in the Library's collections, which include Jacques Lefèvre d'Etaples *Psalterium Quincuplex* of 1509 and a number of editions of the classics, including Horace, Anacreon, and Plutarch. The Library also owns two of the most important books of this period, Guillaume de la

Perrière's *Théâtre des Bons Engins* (Paris: Deny Jarnot, 1539) and Jacques Focard's *Paraphrase de l'Astrolabe* (Lyon: Jean de Tournes, 1546). The *Roman de la Rose* is represented by a number of 16th-century editions and Joachim du Bellay by four 16th-century and two 17th-century editions, including an early (Paris, 1569) edition of *Les Oeuvres Françoises*. One of the gems of this period is the 1547 collection of translations into French by Jacques Peletier, which includes two books of Homer's *Odyssey* and the first book of Virgil's *Georgics*, as well as sonnets by Petrarch and Peletier's ode to Ronsard. Of great importance and rarity is Etienne Jodelle's *Les Oeuvres et Meslanges Poetiques*, published in Paris in 1583, which includes an early essay on the "French poets" by Charles de la Mothe. Original editions of others of the Pléiade, including Remy Belleau, Pontus de Tyard, and Jean-Antoine de Baif, are also represented in the collections.

Michel de Montaigne's *Essays* are available in two editions published during his lifetime (1582, 1588), and in the edition edited by his adopted daughter, Marie de Gournay, in 1595. The Library's collections also include more than sixty subsequent editions, including translations, of the *Essays*, including John Florio's English translation of 1613 and Charles Cotton's of 1685–86. There are nearly 300 titles, including periodicals, of history and criticism on French literature of the 16th century.

The 17th Century

The Library has extensive collections in 17th-century French literature. There are editions from 1615 and 1616 of the "Huguenot Bible" with the Psalms translated by Clément Marot and Théodore de Bèze, as well as later, separate publications of these poems. The three-volume collection of Corneille, published in 1660 with celebratory, theoretical prefaces, is among the most important titles, as are the exceedingly rare editions of his *La Suivante* (1637) and *Oedipe* (1659). Molière is represented by first editions of *Le Misanthrope* (Paris, 1672) and *Les Femmes Sçavantes* (Paris, 1673), as well as the Amsterdam editions of *Le Malade Imaginaire*, published partially in 1673 and fully in 1674. There are also several early translations, versions, or adaptations of Molière into English including those by Dryden, Shadwell, and Roger L'Estrange. Racine is represented by 17th-century editions of *Athalie* and *Esther*, as well as collected works from 1679 and 1690, but not that published by Barbin in the earlier part of the 1670s. The collections also contain first editions of both Pascal's *Pensées* (1670) and his *Provincial Letters* (1659). Each of these authors and most of their works are represented by multiple editions from the 18th, 19th, and 20th centuries, in French, English, and other languages as well (there are more than 180 different editions of Corneille,

280 of Racine, and 605 of Molière).

Other highspots of the 17th century include the very rare Paris and Trévoux editions of Charles Perrault's *Histoires ou Contes du Temps Passé* (1673), Nicolas Boileau Despréaux' *Oeuvres Diverses* (Paris, 1674), and the corrected issue of the first edition of La Rochefoucauld's *Reflexions ou Sentences et Maximes Morales* (Paris, 1665). The Library's Spencer Collection is home to one of the rare first (1668) editions of La Fontaine's *Fables*, with the illustrations intact. The more than 160 later editions owned by the Library include a great variety of 18th-century illustrated versions. As to Madeleine, Madame de Scudéry there is, unfortunately, no first edition of her "novel" *Clélie*, though there is a 1678 translation into English. However, the 1678 edition, published anonymously, of Madame de La Fayette's *La Princesse de Clèves* is one of the Library's great treasures. There are two copies of Charles Perrault's two-volume summing up of the century in engravings, *Les Hommes Illustrés* (1696–1700), as well as a set of the twenty-three volumes of Louis XIV's engraved *Cabinet du Roi*, published by the Imprimerie Royale from 1679 to 1743.

Voltaire and the 18th Century

Although the Library owns several late 18th-century, multivolume sets of the *Letters* of Madame de Sévigné, as well as more than fifty modern editions, it does not own copies of the early editions published between 1725 and 1754. The Library owns a fine copy of the first edition of Montesquieu's *De l'Esprit des Loix* (Geneva, 1748), and two copies of the famed *Encyclopédie* (1776–77). There are several important collections of French Revolutionary pamphlets and *Mazarinades*, as well as numerous legal collections and volumes of laws and acts.

The Library's outstanding and unique Voltaire collection — including well over 2,000 titles by and about Voltaire — is probably the most complete in North America due to the recent addition of the Martin Gross Collection. For instance, the Library now has all but one of the editions of *Candide* published during the author's lifetime.

Rousseau is represented in the catalog by nearly 400 entries, including first editions of both *Julie, ou La Nouvelle Heloïse* (Amsterdam, 1761) and *Émile, ou De l'Éducation* (Amsterdam, 1762), as well as three multivolume collected works printed in Paris and Geneva in the late 18th century. There is also a good collection of early English translations of these and other works and nearly a thousand volumes of criticism, interpretation, and biography.

The 19th Century

The Library has decent collections of the great French novelists of the 19th century — Balzac, Hugo, Stendhal, and Zola — as well as an outstanding collection of the works of Anatole France. For these authors there are also large collections of critical and biographical works. In addition, the Library owns a large collection of the works of Chateaubriand including his ur-collective work *Génie du Christianisme*. For Balzac, there are two of the "Complete Works" published in the late 19th century (1842–48 and 1869–76) but not the earlier and lesser collection published in 1836–40 under the pseudonym Horace de Saint Aubin. In general, the individual novels are present in early editions, though rarely the first, which is the case for most 19th-century French authors in the collection. There are more than 450 entries in the public catalog for Zola, a little more than 200 for Stendhal, and a surprisingly low number for Flaubert, only a little over 200, though the Library does own a copy of the first edition of *Madame Bovary* (Paris, 1857). There are more than 300 entries in the catalog for the works of Anatole France, which include from the Blumenthal Collection copies of most of the first editions, bound by Gruel.

Maupassant is represented by more than 325 entries. Although there are no first editions, many editions of the late 19th and early 20th centuries are present, including several illustrated texts in the Spencer Collection, the most striking of which is *La Maison Tellier* with illustrations by Edgar Degas (1934).

Representing the early Romantic poets are more than 250 works by Alphonse de Lamartine, including two early editions of *Les Méditations Poétiques* (1823 and 1835) and two early editions of *Harmonies Poétiques et Religieuses* (Brussels, 1835 and 1838). For Théophile Gautier, more than 300 works are listed, but first editions of *Émaux et Camées* (1852) and *Mademoiselle De Maupin* (1835) are not among them. The collection of works by the poet Gérard de Nerval is weak, though there are a plethora of texts and translations in English as well as three editions of his great travel diary, *Voyage en Orient* (1851, 1860, and 1997). There are first editions of *Contes et Facéties* (Paris, 1852), *Les Filles du Feu* (Paris, 1854), and his travel essays, *La Bohème Galante* (Paris, 1855). There are two versions of *Aurélia* in the original French as well as four English translations and one into German. The Library does not own the first edition of Nerval's best-known work, *Les Chimères*, but has four modern French editions including the one published in 1944 by Les Amis de Poésie, with lithographs by Moreau. The collection of works by the magnificently eccentric Comte de Lautréamont is unaccountably weak. There are no original editions, but there are several translations into English, as well as translations into Czech, Spanish, and Swedish. Probably the most interesting items are a reprint (Paris, 1946), edited by Philippe Soupault, of the *Oeuvres*

Complètes of 1927. The Music Division holds some interesting manuscripts of John Cage that are based on *Les Chants de Maldoror*. The Spencer Collection has the 1934 edition with illustrations by Salvador Dalí.

With the exception of Mallarmé, the giants of the late 19th century are better represented in the collections. The major work there of Mallarmé is his 1875 translation of Poe's "The Raven," with illustrations by Manet. The Library also holds the 1887 edition of *L'Après-midi d'un Faune* with frontispiece and decorations by Manet, as well as the 1943 Neuchâtel facsimile of the 1914 edition of *Un Coup de Dés*. The Spencer Collection has copies of Mallarmé's *Pages* with a frontispiece etching by Renoir (Brussels, 1891), *Madrigaux* with illustrations by Raoul Dufy (Paris, 1920), and *Poésies*, with illustrations by Matisse (Lausanne, 1932). For Baudelaire, there are nearly 100 editions of *Les Fleurs du Mal*, including two copies of the first edition (1857) and one of the augmented version of 1861. The 1917 edition, edited by Apollinaire, is present, as are the translations by Roy Campbell, Wallace Fowlie, and Edna St. Vincent Millay. The Henry W. and Albert A. Berg Collection of English and American Literature has manuscripts of Millay's translations as well as of some cooperative translations by May Sarton and Muriel Rukeyser. The grand editions of *Les Fleurs du Mal* with illustrations by Rodin (1918) and Matisse (1947) are in the Spencer Collection. The Library has first editions of all five of Baudelaire's translations of Poe.

The collections include more than 150 different versions of Rimbaud's writings, including translations. There is a first edition of *Une Saison en Enfer* (Brussels, 1873). Although the Library does not own a first edition of *Les Illuminations* (1886), the Spencer Collection has the edition illustrated by Leger, published in 1949, as well as the *Poésies* of 1895. The Library owns very few of the individual volumes of Verlaine in their first editions, but many later editions of each (nearly 150 different versions, including musical settings). In addition, most but not all of the complete works and various other collected versions of poems and prose are held. The Spencer Collection owns the Vollard editions of *Parallèlement* (1900) and *Sagesse* (1911) with illustrations by Pierre Bonnard and Maurice Denis, respectively.

The 20th Century

There are no real rarities in the Library's collection of over 200 works by Proust. The earliest edition of his masterwork, *À la Recherche du Temps Perdu*, owned by the Library is that published by Gallimard beginning in 1919. The Berg Collection has Vladimir Nabokov's teaching copy of the Modern Library edition of C. K. Scott Moncrieff's translation of *Swann's Way* (1928). The more than 800 entries for materials about Proust include one hundred on *À la Recherche du Temps Perdu* alone.

Also standing at the beginning of the century is Paul Valéry, represented in the catalog by more than 240 entries for works by him and 370 for works about him. Of greatest interest are the first edition of *La Jeune Parque* (1917) along with several illustrated versions and several presentation copies. Paul Claudel, Francis Carco, Valery Larbaud, Charles Peguy, and other more conservative writers of the early part of the century are also represented at this level. Later novelists are perhaps less well represented, except for the new novelists such as Alain Robbe-Grillet, for whom there are more than fifty titles, including first editions of all his works. There are more than 120 catalog entries for works by Marguerite Duras, fifty-one for Nathalie Sarraute, and thirty-five for Claude Simon. Michel Butor is represented by more than 170 works, including, of course, his letters, essays, art writing, and criticism, as well as several collaborations on artist's books.

The Library's 20th-century collections are extensive and special due to the holdings of the Spencer Collection of Illustrated Books and Fine Bindings. This collection has an extensive representation of the production of French book artists and, as a result, a variety of editions of the works of French writers, primarily poets. In addition, the recently acquired Elaine Cohen Dada Collection contains more than 300 items, some of them very rare or ephemeral. The collection of surrealist books, acquired over the years, is also very strong, with a concentration of materials by Max Ernst.

The new poetry began with Guillaume Apollinaire, who is extensively represented by more than 180 entries, including first editions of *Alcools* (1913), *Les Peintres Cubistes* (1913), and his other early art writings, as well as a copy of the two-volume collection of works of Pietro Aretino published by the Bibliothèque des Curieux in 1909–10, which includes Apollinaire's introduction. Other early volumes include Apollinaire's edition of the works of Baudelaire (1917) and the first edition of the famed *Les Mamelles de Tirésias* (1918). The Spencer Collection contains *L'Enchanteur Pourrissant*, illustrated with wood engravings by André Derain (1909), *Le Bestiaire*, with wood engravings by Raoul Dufy (1911), *Le Poète Assassiné*, with lithographs by Dufy (1926), and *Calligrammes*, with lithographs by De Chirico (1930). Another 240 entries in the catalog list material on Apollinaire.

As a bridge between Dada and Surrealism, the collection of materials by Tristan Tzara is very strong and includes first editions of nearly all his work, most remarkably, *La Première Aventure Céleste de Monsieur Antipyrine* (Zurich, 1916), *Vingt-cinq Poèmes* (Zurich, 1918), *Sept Manifestes Dada* (1924), *Mouchoir de Nuages* (1925), and *Où Boivent les Loups* (1932). Max Jacob's work, also difficult to classify, is unusually well represented, with an excellent 1911 copy of *Saint*

Matorel, with illustrations by Picasso, as the centerpiece.

The collection of materials by the surrealist mage André Breton is equal to that of Apollinaire, and includes five issues of the periodical *Le Surréalisme* (1956–59) as well as many first editions. Some of the most important items include first editions of *Les Champs Magnétiques* (1920), *Le Surréalisme et la Peinture* (1928), *Ralentir Travaux* (1930), and *Violette Nozières* (1933); the *View* magazine edition of *Young Cherry Trees Secured Against Hares* (New York, 1946); a copy of the "catalog" for the Exposition internationale du surréalisme, *Le Surréalisme en 1947* (Paris: Maeght, 1947); *Au Lavoir Noir*, with artwork by Marcel Duchamp (Paris, 1956); and Man Ray's *La Photographie N'est Pas l'Art*, with Breton's introduction (Paris, 1937). Collections for other surrealists, including Philippe Soupault, Robert Desnos, and Louis Aragon, are similarly composed.

Francis Ponge is well represented by more than sixty items, including *Douze Petits Ecrits* (1926), *Le Parti Pris des Choses* (1942), *L'Oeillet. La Guêpe. Le Mimosa* (1946), and *Le Savon* (1967). Collections of his work include those published by Gallimard in 1961, 1965, 1991, and 1997, as well as those edited by Philippe Sollers (1963; new edition, 2001) and Jean Thibaudeau (1967; new edition, 1992). The Library also has the diaries of 1992 and several collections of letters, to Thibaudeau (1998) and Jean Tortel (1999). The Spencer Collection has two rare items: *Cinq Sapates*, with watercolors by Georges Braque (Paris, 1950), and *Matière et Mémoire*, with illustrations by Jean Dubuffet (Paris, 1945).

The collection of poetry from mid-century and beyond is particularly good for the more philosophical, experimental, and avant-garde poetries. There are, for instance, sixty entries for Philippe Sollers, fifty for André Du Bouchet, forty for Marcelin Pleynet, and twenty for Denis Roche. Other contemporary authors include Eugène Guillevic with sixty-three entries, Yves Bonnefoy with ninety-eight, Edmond Jabès with sixty-five, Philippe Jaccottet with fifty-five, Emmanuel Hocquard with twenty, and Christophe Tarkos with eight.

There are more than a thousand literary periodicals in the collections, including runs of *Revue de Paris* (1853–56, 1894–1970), *Mercure de France* (1890–1920), *Revue des Deux Mondes* (1829–1941), *La Nouvelle Revue Française* (1909–43), *La Revolution Surréaliste* (1924–29, microfilm), *Le Surréalisme* (1956–59), *Tel Quel* (1960–82), *Action Poétique* (1955–present), *Java* (1989–present), and, in fact, most if not all of the contemporary journals listed in this work, including a link in the online catalog to *Double Change*.

New York, July 2002

Bibliography

GENERAL

La Bibliothèque Nationale de France. <http://www.bnf.fr/>

Dictionnaire des lettres françaises: Le XXe siècle. Martine Bercot and André Guyaux, eds. Paris: Librairie Générale Francaise, 1998.

Fauchereau, Serge. *Paris–New York: Échanges littéraires au XXe siècle.* Paris: Centre Georges Pompidou/Bibliothèque publique d'Information, 1977.

Library of Congress Online Catalogues. <http://www.loc.gov/catalog/>

1850–1900 / Early Encounters

Albert, Pierre. *La France et les États-Unis et leur Presses, 1632–1976.* Paris: Centre National d'Art et de Culture Georges Pompidou, 1977.

Baudelaire, Charles. *Œuvres complètes.* Paris: Bibliothèque de la Pléiade, 1975.

———. *Selected Letters of Charles Baudelaire: The Conquest of Solitude.* Translated and edited by Rosemary Lloyd. Chicago: University of Chicago Press, 1986.

Carlson, Eric W. *Critical Essays on Edgar Allan Poe.* Boston: G.K. Hall & Co., 1987.

Erkkila, Betsy. *Walt Whitman Among the French: Poet and Myth.* Princeton: Princeton University Press, 1980.

Gourmont, Remy de. *Les Petites Revues. Essai de bibliographie.* Paris: Librairie du Mercure de France, 1900. (Réédition Paris: Ent'revues, 1992).

Larbaud, Valery. *Ce vice impuni, la lecture. Domaine anglais.* Béatrice Mousli, ed. Paris: Gallimard, 1998.

Lawler, James. *Edgar Poe et les poètes français.* Paris: Julliard, coll. Conférences essais et leçons du Collège de France, 1989.

Lemmonier, Léon. *Edgar Poe et les poètes français.* Paris: Editions de la Nouvelle Revue Critique, 1932.

Making of America. Cornell University & University of Michigan. <http://moa.cit. cornell.edu/moa/index.html & http://www.umdl.umich.edu/moa>

Mott, Franck Luther. *A History of American Magazines.* Cambridge: Harvard University Press, 1968, 5 volumes.

Tebbel, John. *The American Magazine: A Compact History.* New York: Hawthorn Books, Inc., 1969.

Valéry, Paul. *Leonardo Poe Mallarmé*. Translated by Malcolm Cowley and James R. Lowler. Princeton: Princeton University Press, 1972.

———. *Lettres à quelques-uns*. Paris: Gallimard, 1952.

Vines, Lois Davis. *Valéry and Poe, a Literary Legacy*. New York: New York University Press, 1992.

Wells, Daniel A. *The Literary Index to American Magazines, 1815–1865*. Metuchen & London: The Scarecrow Press, 1980.

Whitman, Walt. *Oeuvres choisies*. Paris: Gallimard, 1918.

Williams, William Carlos. *In the American Grain*. New York: New Directions, 1956.

1900–1920 / Paris, NY

The Armory Show. May 2001. University of Virginia. <http://xroads.virginia.edu/~MUSEUM/Armory/armoryshow.html>

Baldwin, Neil. *Man Ray: American Artist*. New York: Clarkson N. Potter, Inc., 1988.

de Zayas, Marius. *How, When, and Why Modern Art Came to New York*. Francis M. Naumann, ed. Cambridge, Mass., and London, England: The MIT Press, 1996.

Foresta, Merry. *Perpetual Motif: The Art of Man Ray*. Washington, D.C.: National Museum of American Art/New York: Abbeville, 1988.

Naumann, Francis M. *New York Dada 1915–1923*. New York: Abrams, 1994.

"Rarities from 1917: Facsimiles of *The Blind Man* No. 1, *The Blind Man* No. 2 and *Rongwrong*" (Marcel Duchamp, Henri-Pierre Roché and Beatrice Wood, eds.). Compiled by Thomas Girst. *tout-fait: The Marcel Duchamp Studies On-Line Journal* 1.3 (Dec. 2000) <http://www.tout fait.com/issues/issue_3/Collections/girst/index.html>

Richter, Hans. *Dada: Art and Anti-Art*. London: Thames and Hudson, Ltd., 1965

Sanouillet, Michel. *Dada à Paris. Nouvelle édition revue et corrigée*, établie par Anne Sanouillet. Paris: Flammarion, 1993.

———. *391*. Vol. 1: Réedition intégrale de la revue publiée de 1917 à 1924 par Francis Picabia. Paris: Le Terrain Vague, 1960. Vol. 2: *Francis Picabia et « 391 »*. Paris: Éric Losfeld, 1966.

Schwarz, Arturo. *Man Ray: The Rigour of Imagination*. New York: Rizzoli, 1977.

1920–1930 / The Here of There

Beach, Sylvia. *Shakespeare & Company*. Lincoln: University of Nebraska Press, 1991.

Centre Culturel Américain. *Les Années Vingt. Les Écrivains Américains à Paris et leurs Amis 1920–1930*. Exposition du 11 Mars au 25 Avril 1959. Paris: Les Presses artistiques, 1959.

Ford, Hugh. *Four Lives in Paris*. With a foreword by Glenway Wescott. San Francisco: North Point Press, 1987.

———. *Published in Paris: A Literary Chronicle of Paris in the 1920s and 1930s*. Foreword by Janet Flanner. New York: Collier Books, Macmillan Publishing Company, 1975.

In transition: A Paris Anthology. Writing and Art from transition Magazine 1927–1930. With an introduction by Noel Riley Fitch. London: Secker & Warburg, 1990.

Jolas, Eugene. *Man from Babel*. Edited, annotated, and introduced by Andreas Kramer and Rainer Rumold. New Haven: Yale University Press, 1998.

Joost, Nicholas. *Scofield Thayer and The Dial, an Illustrated History*. Carbondale and Edwardsville: Southern Illinois University Press, 1964.

———. *Years of Transition: The Dial 1912–1920*. Barre, Massachusetts: Barre Publishers, 1967.

Marek, Jayne E. *Women Editing Modernism: "Little" Magazines & Literary History*. Lexington: University Press of Kentucky, 1995.

Soupault, Philippe. "La Nouvelle littérature américaine." *Europe* 142 (October 1934): 272–279.

Untermeyer, Louis. *Modern American Poetry. A Critical Anthology*. New York: Harcourt, Brace and Company, 1936 (fifth revised edition; first edition in 1919).

Williams, Ellen. *Harriet Monroe and the Poetry Renaissance. The First Ten Years of Poetry, 1912–1922*. Chicago: University of Illinois Press, 1977.

Zingman, Barbara. *The Dial, an Author Index*. Troy, N.Y.: The Whitston Publishing Company, 1975.

1930–1950 / There and Back

Cariguel, Olivier. "Panorama et typologie des revues littéraires légales françaises sous l'Occupation." *La Revue des Revues* 24 (1997): 7–18.

Monnier, Adrienne. *The Very Rich Hours of Adrienne Monnier*. Translated, with an introduction and commentaries by Richard McDougall. New York: Charles Scribner's Sons, 1976.

Noël, Bernard. *Marseilles–New York, a Surrealist Liaison*. Marseilles: André Dimanche éditeur, 1985.

Parrot, Louis. *L'Intelligence en guerre*. Paris: La Jeune Parque, 1945.

View: *Parade of the Avant-garde. An Anthology of View Magazine (1940–1947)*. Charles Henri Ford, ed. New York: Thunder's Mouth Press, 1991.

Vignes, Henri & Jean-Yves Lacroix. *L'Intelligence en guerre: géographie nocturne*. Nîmes: La Palourde & Vignes, 2001.

1950–1970 / Catching Up with Now

Bly, Robert. "Bill Duffy Memoir: Notes on 1957 and '58" Robert Bly. <http://www.robertbly.com/r_e_billduffy.html>

Clay, Steven, and Rodney Phillips. *A Secret Location on the Lower East Side: Adventures in Writing, 1960–1980*. New York: The New York Public Library/Granary Books, 1998.

Corman, Cid. "Communication: Poetry for Radio" (originally published in *Poetry*, October 1952). *Modern & Contemporary American Poetry*. Ed. Al Filreis, English Dept., University of Pennsylvania. <http://www.english.upenn.edu/~afilreis/88/corman-on-radio.html>

———. "Origin." *TriQuarterly* 43 (Fall 1978): 239–247.

Eshleman, Clayton. "Doing Caterpillar." *TriQuarterly* 43 (Fall 1978): 450–471.

Finck, Michèle. "Relations avec les poètes étrangers : traduction, réception." Pp. 63–71 in *Poésie de language française, 1945–1960*. Marie-Claire Bancquart, ed. Paris: Presses universitaires de France, 1995.

Martin, Peter. "An Annotated Bibliography of Selected Little Magazines." *TriQuarterly* 43 (Fall 1978): 666–750.

Paire, Alain. *Chroniques des Cahiers du Sud, 1914–1966*. Paris: IMEC, 1993.

Rosset, Barney, ed. *Evergreen Review Reader 1957–1967*. New York: Grove Press, Inc., 1968.

1970–2002 / From Neo-Past to Post-Present

Boulanger, Pascal. *Une « Action Poétique » de 1950 à aujourd'hui*. Paris: Flammarion, 1998.

Bourgois, Christian. *Christian Bourgois: 1966–1986*. Paris: Christian Bourgois éditeur, 1986.

Duration Press. <http://www.durationpress.com/international/bibliography.htm>

Electronic Poetry Center. <http://epc.buffalo.edu/>

Ent'revues. <http://www.entrevues.org/>

Ent'revues. *Guide des revues sur internet*. Paris: Ent'revues, 2001.

Fauchereau, Serge. *Lecture de la poésie américaine*. Paris: Editions de Minuit, 1968. Edition augmentée et illustrée. Paris: Somogy éditions d'art, 1998.

Fondation Royaumont. *À Royaumont: traduction collective 1983–2000*. Grane: Éditions Créaphis, 2000.

Grégoire, Bruno. *Poésies aujourd'hui*. Paris: Seghers, 1990.

Hocquard, Emmanuel et Raquel. *Orange Export Ltd.: 1969–1986*. Paris: Flammarion, 1986.

"The Little Magazine in America: A Modern Documentary History. Essays, Memoirs, Photo-Documents, an Annotated Bibliography." *TriQuarterly* 43 (Fall 1978).

"La poésie au format *Zuk*: Entretien avec Claude Royet-Journoud." *La Revue des revues* 5 (Spring 1988): 72–74.

Revues en vue: Les revues de création littéraire françaises. Thierry Guichard, ed. Besançon: Centre Régional du Livre Franche-Comté, 2000.

Timeline

1815   *North American Review* is founded in Iowa.

1832   *Revue des Deux Mondes* is founded in Paris.

1834   *The Literary Messenger* is founded in Richmond, Virginia.

1837   April: An anonymous essay on "Modern French Poetry" appears in the *North American Review.*

1844   *La Revue de Paris* is founded in Paris.

1845   Anonymous translations of Poe's "The Purloined Letter" and "The Descent into the Maelstrom" appear in *Le Magasin Pittoresque* and *La Revue Britannique,* respectively.

1846   October: "Les Contes d'Edgar A. Poe," by E.D. Forgues, appears in the *Revue des Deux Mondes.*

1847   January: Poe's "The Black Cat," translated by Isabelle Meunier, appears in *La Démocratie Pacifique.*

1850   Harper's *New Monthly Magazine* is founded in New York.

1852   March & April: "Edgar Allan Poe, sa vie et ses ouvrages," by Charles Baudelaire, appears in the *Revue de Paris.*

1853   *Putnam's Monthly* is founded in New York.

1855   Whitman's *Leaves of Grass* is published.

1857   Baudelaire's *Les Fleurs du Mal* is published.

1861   November: "Walt Whitman, poète philosophe et *rowdy*," by Louis Etienne, appears in *La Revue Européenne.*

1864   August: "Edgar Poe d'après ses poésies," by Armand Renaud, appears in the *Revue de Paris.*

1872   June: "Un poète américain — Walt Whitman; 'Muscle and Pluck Forever,' " by Thérèse Bentzon, appears in the *Revue des Deux Mondes.*

        Summer: A selection of poems by Poe, translated by Stéphane Mallarmé, appears in *La Renaissance littéraire et artistique.*

"La Poésie en Angleterre et aux États-Unis," by Emile Blémont, appears in *La Renaissance littéraire et artistique*.

1875   *La République des Lettres* is founded in Paris by Catulle Mendès.

1876   A selection of poems by Poe, translated by Stéphane Mallarmé, appears in *La République des Lettres*.

1883   April: "The Genius of Lamartine," by F.V. Paget, appears in the *Overland Monthly and Out West Magazine*.

1885   July: "Victor Hugo," by F.V. Paget, appears in the *Overland Monthly and Out West Magazine*.

1886   June: "Brins d'herbe: traduit de l'étonnant poète américain Walt Whitman," by Jules Laforgue, appears in *La Vogue*.

1888   November: "Walt Whitman — Poèmes," translated by Francis Viélé-Griffin, appears in the *Revue Indépendante*.

1889   *La Revue Blanche* is founded in Paris.

1890   *Mercure de France* is founded in Paris.

1893   March: "The French Symbolists," by Aline Gorren, appears in *Scribner's Magazine*.

1903   *Camera Work* is founded in New York by Alfred Stieglitz.

1905   December: "Walt Whitman: Poèmes," translated by Louis Fabulet, appears in *L'Ermitage*.

1908   Publication of the biography *Walt Whitman, l'homme et son œuvre*, by Léon Bazalgette.

1909   Publication of Walt Whitman's *Feuilles d'Herbe*, translated by Léon Bazalgette.

        "Walt Whitman en français," by Valery Larbaud, appears in *La Phalange*.

1912   October: *Poetry: A Magazine of Verse* is founded in Chicago by Harriet Monroe.

1914   *The Little Review* is founded in Chicago by Margaret C. Anderson.

1915   March: *291* is founded in New York by Marius de Zayas and Paul B. Haviland.

Publication of the first and only issue of *The Ridgefield Gazook*, edited by Man Ray.

November 15th: Adrienne Monnier opens La Maison des Amis des Livres in Paris, at 7 rue de l'Odéon.

391 is founded in Barcelona by Francis Picabia.

1916   May: The first and only issue of *Cabaret Voltaire* is published in Zurich by Hugo Ball.

La Revue Européenne is founded in Geneva by André Germain.

1917   April 10: Publication of the first issue of *The Blindman*, edited by Marcel Duchamp, Henri-Pierre Roché and Beatrice Wood.

Picabia publishes issues 5-7 of *391* in New York.

Publication of the first and only issue of *Rongwrong*, edited by Marcel Duchamp, Henri-Pierre Roché and Beatrice Wood.

1918   Publication of Walt Whitman's *Oeuvres Choisies*, with translations by Jules Laforgue, Louis Fabulet, André Gide, Valery Larbaud, Jean Schlumberger, Francis Viélé-Griffin.

1919   March: Publication of the first and only issue of *TNT*, edited by Man Ray.

November 17th: Sylvia Beach opens Shakespeare & Co. in Paris, at 8 rue Dupyutren, moving to 12 rue de l'Odéon in July 1921.

Publication of *Modern American Poetry*, edited by Louis Untermeyer.

1921   September: "Renaissance de la poésie américaine," by Valery Larbaud, appears in the *Revue de France*.

Publication of the first and only issue of *New York Dada*, edited by Marcel Duchamp and Man Ray.

Gargoyle is founded in Paris by Arthur Moss.

1922   February: Joyce's *Ulysses* is published by Shakespeare & Co. in Paris.

May 31st: Paul Valéry gives his first public talk (on the "Ideas of Edgar Poe") at the Maison des Amis des Livres.

1923   *Europe* is founded in Paris by Romain Rolland.

1924   January: *The Transatlantic Review* is founded in Paris by Ford Madox Ford.

Commerce is founded by Marguerite Caetani.

1925   *Le Navire d'Argent* is founded in Paris by Adrienne Monnier.

1926   *This Quarter* is founded in Paris by Ethel Moorhead and Ernest Walsh.

March: Special issue of *L'Ane d'Or*: "Walt Whitman."

1927   Fall: Poe's "Marginalia," translated by Paul Valéry, appears in *Commerce*.

transition is founded in Paris by Eugene Jolas.

The Exile is founded in Dijon by Ezra Pound.

1928   Publication of *Anthologie de la Nouvelle Poésie Américaine*, edited by Eugene Jolas.

1929   *Bifur* is founded in Paris by Nino Franck and Georges Ribemont Dessaignes.

Échanges is founded in Paris by Allanah Harper.

Tambour is founded in Paris by Harold J. Samuelson.

1931   *The New Review* is founded in Paris by Samuel Putnam.

La Revue du Monde Noir / The Review of the Black World is founded in Paris by Paulette and Andrée Nardal.

1934   October: "La nouvelle littérature américaine," by Philippe Soupault, appears in *Europe*.

1935   *Mesures* is founded in Paris by Henry Church.

1938   *Fontaine* is founded in Algiers by Max-Pol Fouchet.

1939   *Poètes Casqués* is founded by Pierre Seghers.

1940   *Poésie 40* (then *Poésie 41*, *Poésie 42*, etc.) is founded by Pierre Seghers.

1941   *View Magazine* is founded in New York by Charles Henri Ford.

1942   *VVV* is founded in New York by André Breton.

1943   July: Special issue of *Fontaine*: "Écrivains et poètes des États-unis."

Hemisphères is founded in New York by Yvan Goll.

Special issue of *Messages*: "Domaine français."

1944   June: *L'Eternelle Revue* is founded in Paris by Paul Eluard.

1945   October: Special issue of *Poetry*: "Poets of the French Occupation and Resistance."

1946   March: Special issue of *View*: "View Paris."

1947   Publication of *Anthologie de la poésie américaine contemporaine*, edited by Maurice Le Breton.

1948   Publication of *La Poésie américaine "moderniste," 1910-1940*, edited by Sona Raiziss.

1951   *Origin* is founded by Cid Corman.

1952   September: Special issue of *Poetry*: "New French Poetry."

1953   December: *Action Poétique* is founded in Marseilles by Jean Malrieu, Marie-Thérèse Brousse, Gérald Neveu, Nicole Cartier-Bresson, and Jean-Noël Agostini. (Henri Deluy will become editor in 1958.)

        The Paris Review is founded in Paris by Peter Matthiessen and Harold L. Humes.

1954   Publication of *Panorama de la littérature contemporaine aux États-Unis*, by John Brown.

1956   August: Special issue of *Cahiers du Sud*: "Jeune poésie américaine."

        Publication of *Anthologie de la poésie américaine des origines à nos jours*, edited by Alain Bosquet.

1958   *The Fifties* (then *The Sixties* and *The Seventies*) is founded by Robert Bly and William Duffy.

1960   June: Special issue of *Les Lettres Nouvelles*: "Beatniks."

        Publication of *The New American Poetry*, edited by Donald Allen.

1961   *Locus Solus* is founded in France by John Ashbery, Kenneth Koch, Harry Mathews, and James Schuyler.

        Special issue of *The Sixties*: "Fourteen Poets of France."

1963   *Siècle à Mains* is founded in London by Anne-Marie Albiach and Claude Royet-Journoud.

1964   *Art and Literature* is founded in Paris by John Ashbery.

1965   Special issue of *Tri-Quarterly*: "New French Writing."

1967   *Caterpillar* is founded in New York by Clayton Eshleman.

1968   March/April: Special issue of *Les Lettres Nouvelles*: "Cinq poètes américains."

        Publication of *Lecture de la poésie américaine*, by Serge Fauchereau.

1970   The first part of Louis Zukofsky's *"A"*, translated by Anne-Marie Albiach, appears in *Siècle à Mains*, the first poetry by Zukofsky to be published in French translation.

        Invisible City is founded in Los Angeles by Paul Vangelisti and John McBride.

1971   Special issue of *Change*: "Violence II: Ensemble afro-américain."

        Special issue of *Les Lettres Nouvelles*: "41 poètes américains d'aujourd'hui."

1973   Special issue of *Action Poétique*: "Poésies USA."

1974   *The Paris Review* relocates to New York.

1980   Publication of *Vingt poètes américains*, edited by Jacques Roubaud and Michel Deguy.

1981   *Sulfur* is founded in Pasadena, CA, by Clayton Eshleman.

        Special issue of *in'hui*: "William Carlos Williams."

        Special issue of *Doc(k)s*: "Elementar Poetry in USA East & West."

1986   Publication of *21+1 poètes américains d'aujourd'hui*, edited by Emmanuel Hocquard and Claude Royet-Journoud.

        Série d'écriture is founded; initially published by Spectacular Diseases, it has been published by Burning Deck since 1992.

1987   *o-blēk* is founded by Peter Gizzi and Connell McGrath.

        Zuk is founded in Paris by Claude Royet-Journoud.

1988   *Avec* is founded by Cydney Chadwick.

1989   Un Bureau sur l'Atlantique is founded by Emmanuel Hocquard.

Special issue of *Action Poétique*: "États-Unis: Nouveaux poètes."

Java is founded in Paris by Jean-Michel Espitallier.

1990   Summer: Special issue of *Java*: "Objectivistes américains."

1991   Publication of *49+1 nouveaux poètes américains*, edited by Emmanuel Hocquard and Claude Royet-Journoud.

Special issue of *Tyuonyi*: "Violence of the White Page: Contemporary French poetry."

Special issue of *Poésie 91*: "Walt Whitman le passeur."

1993   Format Américain is founded by Emmanuel Hocquard and Juliette Valéry.

1997   Special issue of *Raddle Moon*: "Twenty-two New (To North America) French Poets."

Special issue of *If*: "Spécial Gertrude Stein."

2000   Fall: Special issue of *Poetry*: "Contemporary French Poetry in Translation."

Special issue of *If*: "Spécial Charles Reznikoff."

Double Change is founded by Omar Berrada, Vincent Broqua, Olivier Brossard, Caroline Crumpacker, Marcella Durand, Claire Guillot, Lisa Lubasch, Andrew Maxwell, Juliette Montoriol, Kristin Prevallet, and Jerrold Shiroma.

2001   Summer: Special "French Issue" of *The Germ*.

Special issue of *L'Œil de bœuf*: "John Ashbery."

2002   January: *Issue* is founded in Marseilles by Eric Giraud, David Lespiau and Eric Pesty.

Summer: "ç" founded by Jerrold Shiroma.